TEN GOOD REASONS
to Invest in Canada

Michael B. Decter

Library and Archives Canada Cataloguing in Publication

Decter, Michael B.
    Ten good reasons to invest in Canada / Michael B. Decter.

Includes bibliographical references.
ISBN 978-1-894692-15-1

1. Investments—Canada. 2. Finance, Personal—Canada.
3. Canada—Economic conditions—1991- . I. Title.

HG5152.D44 2008   332.6'0971   C2008-904309-X

Editor: Ann Decter
Copy Editor: Lisa Foad
Cover Design: Riel Roch-Decter
Inside Layout: Heather Guylar

Printed on Enviro Antique paper, 100% post-consumer recycled, chlorine free stock.

*For all those clients who have given me the most valued gift of all
– their trust.*

And, as always, for my children, Riel and Geneviève.

CONTENTS

PREFACE

At the beginning of the 20th century, Sir Wilfred Laurier, Canada's then prime minister, proudly and optimistically proclaimed that the 20th century would belong to Canada. A careful look at the 20th century however, would suggest that it belonged to Britain, America, and briefly, Japan. Further, a scan of world events would suggest that the 21st century may well belong to China, or perhaps China and India, or maybe all four BRIC countries (Brazil, Russia, India and China). It is my contention, however, that the 21st century in fact, belongs to Canada. Our country offers very compelling long-term investment opportunities. Those of us who live in Canada and are reluctant to invest in our own nation should be more confident. There are many reasons why Canada is the right place for Canadians to invest. This book endeavours to describe the best ten. Perhaps Sir Wilfred was not wrong but merely 100 years ahead of his time.

For most of the past three decades, the conventional wisdom offered to Canadian investors has been to invest elsewhere, and in particular, to invest in the United States. This has largely been very good advice: from 1980–2002, U.S. markets significantly outperformed Canadian equity markets. During the last six years, however, a huge reversal has set in. In 2005, American equities were flat. The Toronto market, as measured by the TSX 60, returned 21%.

While it is true that, in 2006, American markets modestly outperformed Canadian markets, when we take into account the U.S.'s declining currency, it is in fact Canadian equity markets that win the race handily. For the first six months of 2008, the Dow Jones sank over 14% while the Toronto market rose 4%. Driven by twin deficits in trade and government budgets, the American dollar has lost a huge portion of its value compared to the Canadian dollar. Worth barely $0.70 USD a few years ago, the Canadian dollar has since risen to par and soared above the formerly mighty American buck — a gain of nearly 50% from its lows!

This book provides a series of careful arguments as to why, at this particular point in time, Canada is a terrific place to invest. The arguments advanced are rooted in the nature of the Canadian economy and our place in a changing world. It is essential to take a prudent and intelligent longer term view of the rationale for such investing. The rationale rests upon an understanding of both the world economy and Canada in the world economy in the 21st century.

For the past decade, I have been Chief Executive Officer of an investment counsel firm, Lawrence Decter Investment Counsel Inc (LDIC). At LDIC, I work closely with a small team of analysts and a trader, hence the "we" throughout this book.

We manage three mutual funds: the Redwood Diversified Equity Fund, the Redwood Diversified Income Fund, and the Redwood Global Small Cap Fund. As well, we manage over 500 individual accounts. In total, we manage over $400 million of our own and other people's money. Over 90% of that money is invested in Canadian equities, income trusts and fixed income securities.

We have done well for our clients by following the advice offered in this book. For a decade, we have "walked the talk," successfully.

Here are ten good reasons why this is the right time to invest in Canada.

Michael B. Decter

THE STRONG FUNDAMENTALS OF THE CANADIAN ECONOMY

I ntroduction: Why Invest in Canada Now?

For thoughtful investors — amateur or professional — Canada offers terrific long-term investment opportunities. These opportunities are rooted in the sensible, courageous decisions made by the Canadian government over a decade ago: they also rest upon events that occurred in the natural history of our planet hundreds of millions of years ago — events that endowed Canada with an abundance of natural resources, such as potash. The spectacular and continuing economic rise of Asia, particularly China and India, is another reason for Canada's potential. The coming together of these three streams of events positions Canada favourably. In an age when energy will be in scarce supply and available only at high prices, Canada benefits from its rich energy endowment. In an age when security is a major concern for many nations and stability is of great importance to investors, Canada's peace and order is very attractive. In an age when China and India are building modern economies and infrastructure, Canada will prosper by supplying these countries with the resources and expertise they will need.

The Economist magazine publishes an annual statistical look at the world economy. In Pocket World in Figures, they cite a few facts about Canada. In 2007, Canada ranked 36th among the nations of the world in population. Our territory is vast: we are the second largest country in the world after Russia. We are a larger land mass than the United States, which holds ten times our population, or China, which boasts over forty times our population. We are a sparsely populated nation sitting on a vast storehouse of resources.

Canada punches way above our population weight in energy. We were the largest uranium producer in the world, the 3rd largest producer of natural gas and 7th largest producer of oil. In fact, according to *The Economist*'s 2007 stats, we ranked 6th overall as an energy producer. Canada also ranked 9th in overall economic terms. We were 2nd in nickel production, 5th in zinc production, 6th in silver and lead production, and 8th in copper, silver and gold production. Geology and history have been generous to Canada.

One thesis of this book is that the growth in the economies of China and India has important implications for Canada. The demands of these economies for copper, zinc, nickel, potash, uranium, and other commodities, will benefit Canada. Demands of the American economy for natural gas and oil from secure continental sources are a further addition to the arguments. Canada has laid the groundwork for prosperity by putting its fiscal house in order over the last decade. Surpluses in government coffers will allow, in the coming decade, for important investments to be made in education and healthcare, so that these essential services can be modernized — with little likelihood of needing to resort to higher taxation on businesses or individuals. These are the basic foundations for Canada's century, discussed in the first section of this book: The Strong Fundamentals of the Canadian Economy.

The political decisions and events which underpin Canada's recent success have very deep roots. Canada's successful decade-long struggle to move away from a high-deficit, high-debt pattern is set out in Chapter 1. The natural endowments in Canada that will benefit investors were laid down many hundreds of millions of years ago. The oil sands of Alberta, as well as the conventional oil and gas deposits that characterize the Western Canadian Sedimentary Basin, are ancient in origin. Although its heart is in Alberta, the Western Basin, rich in oil and gas, extends well into Saskatchewan and British Columbia. These matters are described in Chapters 2-4. The constitutional principles that underlie Canada and Canada's relative tranquility over the last 200 years are described in Chapter 5. So, too, is Canadian medicare, a benefit to business and investors, as well as all Canadians. Canada's proximity to China with only the Pacific Ocean between us and them, and their seemingly inexhaustible demand for resources such as energy and metals, is reviewed in Chapter 6. The uniquely privileged Canadian position in uranium is tackled in Chapter 7.

Chapter 8 examines opportunity in the real estate investment sector. Canada's stability, as well as its attractiveness to immigrants, renders real estate a solid investment. Chapter 9 takes up the utility of utilities. Those who invest in Canada have an opportunity to benefit from the stability and quality of Canadian utilities. In sectors such as electric power generation and telecommunications, Canadian utilities represent solid long-term value. Canada also offers opportunities in the financial sector, both in banks and non-banks, such as Power Corporation and Manulife Financial. These opportunities are explored in Chapter 10. In Chapter 11, transportation, made necessary by the vastness of our land and the export oriented nature of our economy, is examined from an investment standpoint. There are good investments to be made in transportation manufacturers as well as in enterprises that operate transport. Finally, agriculture and potash are the focus of Chapter 12, with an emphasis on food and fertilizer.

The second section of the book, Making Your Investment, is devoted to how to invest in Canada. There are a number of ways to invest. Picking the right method is important. Chapters 13 and 14 help you decide whether to go it alone or seek the benefit of an experienced professional. Chapter 15 discusses RRSPs, a core investment for many Canadians. And because all advice needs balance, Chapter 16 reviews the risks to the rosy future that has been discussed. Every silver lining has a dark cloud and these clouds are well worth exploring. Investors need to fully evaluate the risks, associated with potential investments, and compare these risks against the opportunities. As always, those investing need to retain responsibility for their choices.

The world economy is undergoing a fundamental shift. The terms of trade, which, for many decades, ran against those who produce and export natural resources, have shifted dramatically back to the natural resource sector. Simply put, resources such as oil, gas, uranium, copper, and potash, are in scarce supply and as such, expensive. This is good news for Canada. It is not the only reason to favour investing in Canada at this time, but it does provide powerful grounds. If you are an investor who believes that oil will return to $10 per barrel, and that natural gas will be available at $2 per McF, that there will be no shortages in the supply of copper, uranium, nickel, potash, coal and other essential commodities, and that China and India will fail to grow — stop reading. If, however, you share my view that energy and resources will be in great demand over the next decade, read on!

The World Needs More Canada

Canada's dominant bookstore chain, Indigo Books, was built by a dynamic entrepreneur, Heather Reisman. Prominently displayed in Indigo stores is the corporate motto, "The World Needs More Canada," along with the names of many Canadian literary icons. Happily, it is true that Canadian authors such as Margaret Atwood, Robertson Davies, Farley Mowat, Pierre Berton, Alice Munro, Michael Ondaatje, Carol Shields, and many others, have become popular around the world. As well, talented Canadians from Anne Murray to Shania Twain to Jim Carrey and Mike Myers entertain the world.

It is also true that the world needs more Canadian resources. It needs our oil, natural gas, coal, uranium, copper, zinc and potash. The world also needs Canada to grow more food. The world needs the talents of our people. That talent is embodied in Canadian universities teaching tens of thousands of overseas students, embodied in technology such as the BlackBerry and in engineering firms such as SNC-Lavalin. "The world needs more Canada" is not only a statement that the world needs more of our cultural output — it is a statement that confidently gestures to Canada's very bright future. For investors, the phrase translates into opportunities to participate by buying shares of Canadian companies such as PotashCorp, Teck Cominco, Barrick Gold, CN (Canadian National), Canadian Pacific Railway (CPR), and dozens of others. Throughout the book, broad ideas are commingled with specific investment opportunities. But be forewarned: we live in rapidly moving markets. A study of the 1970 *Fortune 500* list reveals that one third of the companies on the 1970 list disappeared by 1983, including Alcan, Inco, Algoma, Stelco, Falconbridge, and Alliance Atlantis. By the time this book is published, many of the specific companies that I mention may be gone, taken private or acquired by competitors. Some may be wounded by bad management or changes in their markets. A strong word of caution is appropriate with regard to individual equities. This book is not recommending that you rush out and buy each and every one of the equities mentioned — or that you buy any of them, for that matter. Do your own homework. Even good investments can become overpriced. Be patient about buying as well as selling. At the back of this book is a Resources section to assist your further research. Treat this Top 50 list as a start rather than an end point in your research. Also included as an appendix is our top 45 growing companies list – dubbed the Canadian Future 45. With these smaller companies, you really need to do your homework carefully. Still, on that list may be a future Magna International, Research in Motion or Teck Cominco.

Investment Philosophy

Movies should be exciting. The theatre should challenge and engage you. The symphony and the ballet should make your heart soar. But when it comes to the investment of your hard-earned savings, boring and profitable should trump exciting every time. The successful building of your investment portfolio should not be like a roller coaster ride at the fair. It should be a slow, careful channelling of your savings into solid, perhaps dull investments, that gradually appreciate in value. As will be noted in Chapter 9, several of these "boring" companies have vastly outperformed the over-hyped torpedo stocks of the tech and other mini-booms.

In the fabled race between the tortoise and the hare, the tortoise, slow and steady, always wins. In the important challenge of building your wealth for retirement, you want to own the tortoise's stocks, not the hare's. Canada, with its 21st century potential for vast prosperity, may be a valued tortoise. One of the secrets of successful investing is to embrace the courage of patience.

Long-Term Investing in Turbulent Times

Many would-be investors are alarmed by the recent volatility of markets. With the advent of television channels and networks devoted to business, there is a real-time urgency to large drops in stock markets. Watching knowledgeable commentators deliver their views on how the Dow Jones, an index of thirty stocks, could drop or jump 1000 points baffles many investors. To succeed, you need to take a long-term view and ignore short-term fluctuations. Buying is, of course, best done on a really bad market day, when you are least confident. Selling is best done on a strong market day. Being contrarian will serve you well.

If you don't have the stomach for volatility, build your portfolio from less volatile stocks such as utilities and other dividend-paying stocks and select income trusts. While not invulnerable to sharp upward and downward movements, the volatility of holdings is dampened by their distributions and dividends. Do not start investing believing you will buy stocks at their all-time lows and sell at their all-time highs. You will not. Solid returns are possible with a long-term view, a willingness to endure fluctuations and well-chosen holdings.

1 The Surplus Twins – Trade and Budget

Once upon a time, and for several decades, Canada had an unsolvable federal budget deficit. We owed a huge and growing debt to foreign countries. We were the poor cousins of the G8 nations. Through the successive governments of prime ministers Pierre Trudeau, Joe Clark and Brian Mulroney, Canada sank deeper into debt each year. Our government borrowed from Canadians by selling us massive quantities of bonds. Our banks, while protesting high interest rates and high government spending, bought those bonds by the boatload and profited from owning them. Canada borrowed heavily from the Americans, the Japanese, the British, and the Swiss. In fact, we borrowed in every market available. In my days in the Government of Manitoba, we even borrowed from Puerto Rican-based pharmaceutical companies and from the legendary Belgian dentists. In short, Canadian governments borrowed everywhere they could. By the early 1990s, Canada had become a serious debtor nation. We owed hundreds of billions of dollars to our own citizens and hundreds billions more to lenders worldwide.

The Surplus Twins – Trade and Budget

When Jean Chrétien brought the Liberal Party back into power in 1993, the Government of Canada was running a $42 billion annual deficit on a total budget of only $160 billion. Budget documents disclosed that were spending $10 for every $7.50 we took in. More importantly, Canada's debt to Gross Domestic Product (GDP) ratio had risen so high that among the industrialized nations, only Italy was in a worse financial position. Simply put, our debts were a large portion of our annual economic output. Canada owed its citizens, and the rest of the world, over $600 billion. Media stories forecasted dire consequences for the country. The Canadian dollar slipped to $0.65 USD. It was a grim time for Canada in world financial markets. Rumours circulated in the media about the possible intervention of the International Monetary Fund (IMF) — a clear, loud signal that a country has failed to manage its financial affairs — and an action that would have been unprecedented in modern industrial democracy. The IMF usually confined its interventions to debtor nations in the developing world. The intervention of the IMF is a very serious matter for any nation. The whisper of an IMF appearance underscored the depth of our troubles. The agency of last resort, its loans carry painful conditions.

Today, Canada is running both a trade and budget surplus. We have the healthiest financial position and the lowest debt to GDP ratio of any of the major G7 nations. In recent years, we have performed better than the United States, the United Kingdom, France, Germany and Japan. In fiscal 2005-06, budget documents reveal that the Harper government directed $13.2 billion of surplus to reduce Canada's national debt to $481.5 billion. In 2006-07, the debt was reduced to $467.3 billion. The surplus of $13.8 billion generated in 2006-07 was used to pay down the federal government debt to $453.5 billion. Under the Harper government, reduced interest payments from debt repayment will be recycled as tax reductions, creating a virtuous cycle. Indeed, for the past three years, Canada has outpaced the United States in growth of real disposable income, retail sales, housing prices and even stock prices. What changed our nation's financial fortunes so dramatically and positively?

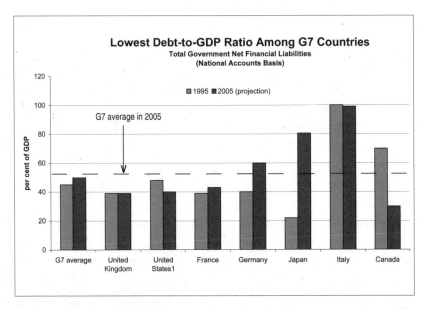

1 Adjusted to exclude certain government employee pension liabilities to improve comparability with other countires' debt measures

Sources: *OECD Economic Outlook*, No. 77 (June 2005); Federal Reserve, *Flow of Funds Accounts of the United States* (June 2006); Department of Finance calculations.

By the 2007 federal budget, Canada's finance minister announced that the target on reducing debt to GDP ratio to below 25% would be delivered by 2011/12, three years ahead of the original target date.

Most of the proper, public credit for engineering the turnaround in Canada's budget situation goes to our finance minister from 1993-2002, Paul Martin. But this achievement was not his alone. To be fair, at least six key players — the "Six Amigos" — participated: Brian Mulroney, Michael Wilson, and Donald Mazankowski; Jean Chrétien, Paul Martin, and David Dodge.

The time frame of the Six Amigos occurred in two phases. From 1994 to 1995, Prime Minister Mulroney's government held office. During this near decade, Mulroney's finance ministers, Michael Wilson and Donald Mazankowski introduced the Goods and Services Tax (GST). They also achieved some expenditure reduction. Prime Minister Chrétien took office in 1993, and appointed Paul Martin, a rival for the prime minister's job, to Finance. There, Minister Martin and Deputy Minister David Dodge formed the team that lead the major expenditure reductions necessary to eliminate Canada's deficits and reduce Canada's debt.

The Mulroney government had run large deficits. However, Prime Minister Mulroney had put into place the hated GST, a national 7% tax with a very broad base. This tax was advertised as revenue neutral with the Manufacturers' Sales Tax (MST) that it replaced. It was not. The GST brought enormous additional revenues to Ottawa. As Mulroney's rich baritone declared a decade later in a taped tribute to Michael Wilson on the occasion of his award from the Public Policy Forum: while "Paul Martin harvested the tulips, it was Mike Wilson who planted the garden!" Not surprisingly, the former prime minister mixed more than a little Irish hyperbole into his assertion. The GST is forecasted to place $34 billion into the federal government's coffers over the next year. Even with the reduction to 6% implemented in the first Harper government budget in 2006, and the subsequent reduction to 5% as of January 1, 2008, the GST remains a huge and incremented revenue source for Ottawa over the MST that it replaced. It is also important to credit Don Mazankowski's unique role of Deputy Prime Minister; "Maz" as he is affectionately known, served as "Chief Operating Officer" of Canada and accomplished much in fixing the Canadian government's chronic overspending.

Ten Good Reasons to Invest in Canada

Canada's Economic and Fiscal Turnaround

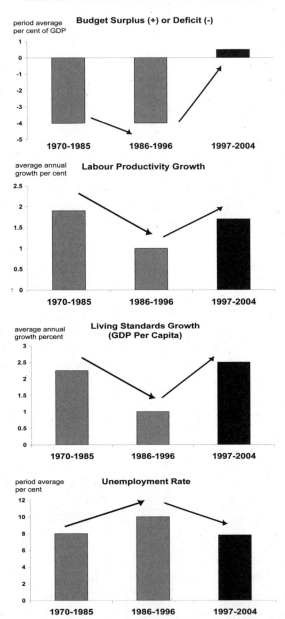

Source: Surplus/Deficit – *Fiscal Reference Tables*, Dept. of Finance Canada (Sept 2005); Labour Productivity – Statistics Canada; Unemployment Rate – Statistics Canada; Labour Force Survey & Historical Statistics Canada (1970-1975); Living Standards – Statistics Canada.

The Surplus Twins – Trade and Budget

Canada's federal finance department has chronicled the turnaround that occurred from 1970-2004. Canada's Economic and Fiscal Turnaround notes four major shifts that capture the dramatic improvement in Canada's economy and finances, including the turn from budget deficit to budget surplus, the gains in labour productivity, and the decline in the unemployment rate. The consequence is a strong gain in living standards as measured by GDP per capita.

One direct payoff of eliminating the deficit and reducing the debt has been lower Canadian interest rates. As Canada proved it was serious about getting its fiscal house in order and about maintaining low and stable inflation through inflation targets, our international fiscal credibility improved, leading to the restoration of the Government of Canada's AAA credit rating, the highest in financial markets. International investors no longer demand a risk premium to hold Government of Canada bonds. This helped to lower all Canadian interest rates because bond rates act as a benchmark for other interest rates in the economy. The key reason for declining interest rates was a global decline in the rate of inflation. Lower interest rates make buying homes and investing in businesses more affordable for Canadians. Similarly, provinces and municipalities have seen their cost of borrowing decline over the past decade. The renewed health of Canada's finances is saving every borrower in Canada some money. Lower interest rates help all the boats float a little higher in the economic pond.

The resolution of Canada's deficit situation, however, required much more than the implementation of the GST. When Chrétien came to power, the deficit was the nation's central problem. Finance Minister Martin found himself with a very able deputy minister, David Dodge. He proved to be a strong supporter for Martin, as he delivered Canada the "cod liver oil" necessary for its economic health. Prime Minister Chrétien was a strong backer who trusted their remedy and could control his caucus. So the second three amigos — Chrétien, Martin and Dodge — undertook the second and essential stage: a significant reduction in the core expenditures of the Government of Canada. They made for an odd combination of talent: Dodge, the cerebral pipe-smoking professor with a Queens and Princeton pedigree; Martin, the son of a powerful cabinet minister who succeeded in business; and Chrétien, the street fighter from Shawinigan. In addition, successive governors of the Bank of Canada, particularly John Crow, assisted with tough-minded policies that quashed Canadian inflation and kept it at bay.

The third ingredient was supplied by the economy itself: very strong economic growth in the mid- to late 1990s, traceable, in part, to the strengthening Asian economy. The massive decline in interest rates offered the necessary last leg in this remarkable turnaround.

Combined, these four factors were a success. The broad GST added new revenue, and government expenditure reductions in transfers and direct government spending meant federal program spending as a percentage of the Canadian economy declined from over 18% in 1983/84 to 12% in 2004–05 as documented in federal budgets. The economy rebounded, led by declining interest rates and exports, some of which were assisted by the North American Free Trade Agreement (NAFTA), another Mulroney government accomplishment.

The sharp decline in interest rates reduced Canada's borrowing cost. A glance at the Bank of Canada's website reveals the plunge in interest rates in the 1990s. In 1990, the Bank of Canada rate had reached 14.05%. By 1991, it declined to 7.67%, and in 1994 it dropped to 3.88%. Since 1994, the rate has not exceeded 8.3%. And, it reached a low of 2.25% in 2002 in the wake of 9/11. A significant portion of the $42 billion federal budget deficit had been interest payments. This declined sharply when Canada was able to refinance its external debt at much lower interest rates. In the single decade from 1994-2004, Canada's annual interest payments on our debt dropped from $49 billion to $34 billion, or 30%. The Department of Finance reports that debt interest payments declined from 40% of federal revenues in 1995-96, to about 17% in 2004/05 — from $0.40 to a mere $0.17 of every dollar of revenue. These powerful forces all moved in the same direction. By the first years of the 21st century, Canada was generating significant budget surpluses at the national level, as well as surpluses, or balanced budgets, in most Canadian provinces. The national political debate shifted dramatically, from feuding over blame for deficits and high unemployment, to the more appealing talk of how to spend the surplus. Despite two back-to-back minority governments, often prone to spending, the federal surplus is intact. The surplus has proven very resilient. Cautious budgeting by Paul Martin as finance minister, and subsequently, prime minister (alongside Finance Minister Ralph Goodale), has allowed for continued annual payments to Canada's total debt, albeit with large spending increases. By 2005, Canada stood alone among the G8 nations with a budgetary surplus.

By mid-2007, despite significant tax cuts by the federal government, massive increases in transfer payments to the provinces, and big increases in government spending, Canada was still running a large surplus. The Harper government's 2006 GST reduction did not dent the surplus for 2007-08. Time will tell whether 2008's GST cut will have the ultimate negative consequences of returning Canada to deficits. Even at 5%, however, the GST is expected to yield over $40 billion in 2009-10 or 15% of the federal government's total revenue. Additionally, while he was finance minister, Paul Martin legislated that any money surplus to budget needs at year-end be used to pay down the government debt. Because of this, actual debt repayment has occurred. The Harper government continued to reduce the national debt through the end of fiscal 2007-08. These repayments, though modest, have contributed to a positive movement in Canada's overall position. Provincial government finances are also in better shape than at any other time. The massive Alberta surplus receives most of the media attention but, as of February 2008, BMO Nesbitt Burns estimates that only the tiny province of Price Edward Island is facing a deficit. Most recently, Newfoundland and Labrador made its entry into the ranks of the "have" provinces, thanks to oil revenues from offshore developments.

Provincial Surpluses (2007/08)

Province	Surplus/deficit in millions of $
Alberta	3,988
Ontario	0
Quebec	0
B.C.	2,125
Saskatchewan	264
Manitoba	298
New Brunswick	79
Nova Scotia	139
Nfld & Labrador	862
Prince Edward Island	-42

Source: Provincial Government Finance, BMO Nesbitt Burns, 2008

The Bank of Canada gradually raised interest rates at 4.5% to dampen inflationary force, but from May 2006 to July 2007, rates held steady. In July 2007, a 0.25% increase was implemented. In the first quarter of 2008, however, interest rate cuts of 0.75% were enacted. More rate cuts may occur to offset an economic slowdown. On the other hand, inflation concerns may cause rates to remain at current levels or rise.

In addition to Canada's budget health at the federal level, Canada is running an enormous trade surplus with its trading partners, in particular the United States. These twin surpluses on the Canadian front come at a time when the American economy has slid into massive twin deficits.

By simultaneously initiating a tax cut and launching the war in Iraq at a cost of some $60-100 billion per year, President George W. Bush achieved what many thought was impossible. In a mere seven years, he moved the U.S. out of the surplus achieved under President Bill Clinton, into a vast deficit. Many of the same reasons that pushed Canada into surplus — low interest rates, economic growth — assisted President Clinton, who managed to put the U.S. on a course of surpluses worth $200-300 billion. President Bush reversed this direction by reducing taxes and fighting an expensive foreign war on borrowed funds. Canada's achievements look all the more positive in contrast to the failures of its major, and much larger, trading partner. At the very time that Canada is running record budget surpluses and engaging in spirited political debate about how to spend them, the United States has returned to record budget deficits, and the debate is one of protectionism. On the trade front, the U.S. has a major trade deficit, largely with China, but also with Canada. Some of this U.S. trade deficit is caused by higher prices for imported oil, but Chinese manufacturing is also rapidly displacing American manufacturing in nearly every sector of the economy.

The short story is, over the past decade, four events have supported Canada's financial turnaround:
- Lower interest rates
- Program spending cuts
- Goods and Services Tax
- Economic growth

For Canada, the current and future economic and fiscal picture is strong. Canada's twin surpluses, coupled with America's twin deficits, have resulted in the steady rise of the Canadian dollar, from the low $0.60 range to parity (plus or minus a few cents). This has been good news for Canadian importers and for those Canadians travelling abroad, but bad news for Canadian exports, which have become more expensive. The higher dollar has started to put real pressure on Canadian manufacturing sectors. Canada is likely to enjoy a strong currency for several years to come. The U.S. dollar could devalue further relative to Euro and Canadian dollars. As we've seen in 2006 and 2007, investments in U.S. dollars may decline even if the underlying investment rises. Putting your investment eggs in an American basket may cause you losses of up to 20% due to devaluation of the U.S. dollar against the Canadian.

These twin surpluses — budgetary and trade — make for the number one reason to invest in Canada. Federal budget surpluses are coupled with massive budget surpluses in Alberta from oil and gas revenue. Improving economic and budgetary fortunes in British Columbia, Saskatchewan, Newfoundland, and Labrador, are also based on oil revenues, though for these provinces, the positive impacts are much less dramatic. The trade surplus is also fueled in part by record prices for oil and other commodity exports, like potash and uranium.

The obvious advantage in investing in a country with an appreciating currency as opposed to one that is depreciating is compelling. But, all silver linings have their inherent black clouds. As the Canadian dollar increases in value relative to the American dollar, our manufacturers are being squeezed. Their products become uncompetitive. Some have been forced to relocate to less expensive nations. Others have closed or bankrupted their companies. Chapter 16 sets out some of the risks to our virtuous investment scenario.

2 Oil Without Wars or Hurricanes – The Alberta Advantage

Canada has vast oil resources. Why is this important? The world needs oil.

The single most influential driver of increased demand for oil is the modernization of transportation in China and the rest of the developing world. The Chinese nation of 550 million bicycle riders is rapidly becoming a nation of car drivers. The 25 million cars on Chinese roads in 2007 is forecast by the World Bank to rise to 140 million by the year 2020. That's nearly 10 million new cars per year. Each and every car will have a fuel tank that will need to be filled, and filled frequently, with gasoline. Even at the level of 140 million cars predicted for 2020, the Chinese will have only one car for each ten people. Right now, in North America, we have one car per person. The appetite for cars is also strong in India where Tata Motors has introduced a Laht car, that at $2,500, could be equivalent to the Ford Model T, an affordable car for the masses. Toyota recently announced a new automobile manufacturing plant to produce 150,000 new small Toyotas per year. Other auto manufactures will follow Toyota's and Tata Motors' example.

As world oil prices skyrocketed above the $140-per-barrel level in mid-2008, visible limitations on the supply of oil became increasingly apparent. There is widespread concern that we are getting close to "peak oil," which means that we are reaching peak productions of oil on a global basis. This does not mean that we can see an exact point wherein we will run out of oil — it describes the point beyond which we will be unable to increase production. Although estimates vary, there is a consensus that oil supply is finite, and peak oil production is expected to hit sometime within the next ten to twenty years. There is even a small but growing group who meet under the banner "Peak Oil" to discuss the concept. T-shirts are included!

Recently, I shared a BNN interview with Gwyn Morgan, the dynamic ex-CEO of EnCana. Morgan knows the energy business as well as anyone in our nation. On the peak oil question, he noted that the world is currently providing and consuming 84 million barrels of oil per day. He was certain that 110-120 million barrels per day — forecasted demand within a few decades — was simply not possible. Seymour Schulich is another Canadian with deep knowledge of the oil and gas business. A billionaire largely due to his investments in oil, Schulich is the author of the recently published best-seller, *Get Smarter*. In his view, "Oil is entering a golden age of shortage of supply. Very tight oil markets will last for the next thirty years to fifty years, until fusion power becomes commoditized" (168).

Further evidence of this reality is that the energy majors, Exxon, Royal Dutch Shell, BP (formerly British Petroleum), and others, are producing less oil than last year, despite much higher prices. This insight is available through a review of their annual reports.

Oil and Instability

A more immediate problem is that most of the world's tradable oil comes from countries with enormous political and economic instability. In his book, *A Thousand Barrels A Second*, Peter Tertzakian captures the realities of world oil supply:

> There are 192 countries in the world, and really all are dependant on oil. On the flip side, only thirty countries produce oil of any significant quantity, and only 17 of them are exporters of oil greater than 500,000 barrels a day. (155)

Of the 17 major oil-exporting nations, many are in politically unstable regions — such as the Middle East. Only two oil exporting nations — Mexico and Canada — share a continent and a land border with the world's largest oil consuming nation, the United States. In 2006, the United States consumed just over 20.5 million barrels of oil per day, while the second largest consumer, China, consumed only 6.7 million barrels per day. However, Chinese oil consumption is growing far faster than North American consumption. Increasingly, Mexico's economic development is requiring domestic consumption. Mexico has moved from exporting to importing natural gas. There are predictions that due to its slowing oil production, Mexico — now the source of 11% of U.S. oil imports — could cease to export within a decade. This would render Canada the sole net supplier of natural gas to America on this continent.

No one needs to be told that the Middle East is not a peaceful region. However, it is a source of much of the world's oil. In 2007, Saudi Arabia was the number one producer in the world, at 10 million barrels per day. An additional 11.7 million barrels per day come from Iraq, Iran, Kuwait and the United Arab Emirates. This represents one quarter of world oil production. The Middle East is a large exporter. Many other nations that produce oil also consume a great deal of their own oil. In addition to the instability in the Middle East, other oil-producing countries, such as Nigeria and Ecuador, are experiencing popular uprisings and insurgents against their governments and oil companies.

Venezuela, a major supplier of oil to the United States, is currently led by President Hugo Chavez, whose political leanings are towards socialism and trade with Latin America. He openly opposes the United States government on most issues. Former American Republican presidential candidate and televangelist, Pat Robertson, suggested, not so long ago, that Chavez should be assassinated. Even though Robertson apologized, this is hardly a basis for improving relations between the U.S. and Venezuela. Chavez's response was to seek oil markets other than those of the United Sates. He remains a volatile player in international politics and oil markets.

The Russian situation is also far from stable, and Russia has provided a great deal of incremental oil to the world in the last two decades. In 2006, it was the second largest producer, at 9.7 million barrels per day, and the second largest exporter, at 6.6 million barrels per day. Also in 2006, President Vladimir Putin put one of his major rivals, the head of a large energy company, in jail, and repatriated control of that company to the state hands. Several multinationals have been forced to surrender projects to Russian control, notably Royal Dutch Shell in Siberia. Foreign capital is very nervous about participating in Russia because of perceived potential instability. As well, the Russian government has "elbowed" its way into ownership of several major energy projects over the past two years. In Russia, the government is the partner of increasingly uneasy multinational corporations. As a consequence, production has been falling in a large number of Russian fields.

In short, oil comes from some of the most troubled parts of the world. Traders and analysts speak of a "political risk premium" in the price of oil, and some estimate this risk of disruption cost to be as high as $25 per barrel. Unless peace is simultaneously established on three troubled continents — a highly unlikely event — a big risk premium will continue.

Then, there's Alberta. Although some dubbed former Premier Ralph Klein, "King Ralph," for his longevity in office, he displayed none of the characteristics of other oil nation rulers. A man of modest tastes, Premier Klein was driven about in a modest car. King Ralph did not have a fleet of Rolls-Royces, or jet airplanes at his disposal. Nor did he employ all of his relatives as princes, or lavish great amounts of oil revenue on family members. Instead, his government sent every Albertan a cheque so everyone could share in the buoyant revenues — one big, happy family. In short, Alberta maintains a modest and efficient administration, one which has been putting its oil money into healthcare services, education, and roads, and into lower taxes. Klein's successor, Ed Stelmach has raised royalties on the oil and gas industry.

During the oil price boom of the 1970s, then-Premier Peter Lougheed made visionary investments in health research that are now paying dividends. Alberta is the only Canadian province without a provincial sales tax, and it has the lowest rate of income tax. In addition to its significant conventional oil and natural gas reserves, Alberta has the tar sands, the largest deposit of extractable oil on earth. When the tar sands oil reserve is counted, Canada joins ranks with the Middle East, in what Prime Minister Stephen Harper has labeled "an energy superpower!" Extracting that resource, however, will test his claim that Canada will become a "clean energy superpower."

In 2007, following massive investments made by other major companies, Royal Dutch Shell committed to a $27 billion investment in the Alberta oil sands. Well over $100 billion of total investment is forecasted for the Alberta oil sands. Some uncertainty has been created by Premier Stelmach's new royalty regime, however, and the longer-term impact of his approach is not yet clear. What is clear is that some energy investment has shifted from Alberta to Saskatchewan and British Columbia.

Just when the world is turning its gaze to Alberta's oil sands, along comes former Vice-President Al Gore to warn of CO_2 emissions and global warming. Alberta and the rest of Canada are in for a prolonged debate between the economic benefits versus environmental impacts of oil sands development. Both local and global aspects of such development are under debate, and Prime Minister Harper, in a minority situation, will endeavour to balance the economic and environmental issues. Other provinces are likely to form alliances, including carbon trading with American states, putting Alberta in a disadvantaged environmental circumstance. The best answer could be new technologies that allow extraction of oil from the sands with less environmental impact.

With regard to economic growth, Alberta's recent performance has been unprecedented. In September 2006, Statistics Canada, in its report, *The Alberta Economic Juggernaut*, noted that no province in Canadian history had recorded growth to rival that experienced recently in Alberta. In just one decade, Alberta's GDP doubled to $66,275 per capita. Further, it achieved the country's highest average hourly earnings ($20.94), the lowest rate of unemployment (2.9%) and the strongest growth in consumer spending.

Alberta's climate could be considered forbidding, with its extreme winter blizzards and 30- and 40-below-zero temperature drops. However, compared to the Gulf of Mexico, Alberta's weather is benign with regard to oil and gas production. The worst intrusion Alberta's weather makes on the exploration and production of oil and gas is that occasionally, an early spring or late fall freeze will make it more difficult to drill on certain lands. Oil and gas facilities tolerate the cold rather well. The turbines that propel natural gas along the pipelines operate better in cold weather than in hot. This is Alberta's advantage over the Gulf of Mexico.

The Gulf took a long time to recover after Hurricane

Katrina battered its oil and gas production facilities. Nine months after Katrina hit, some 25% of the region's gas and oil production was still shut in. In the wake of Hurricane Katrina, BP announced that its 250,000-barrel-per-day Thunder Horse platform would not produce until 2008 — a three-year delay. With changing weather systems, the Gulf of Mexico seems increasingly prone to hurricane damage. Hurricane Ivan struck the Gulf in 2004, destroying seven shallow water drilling platforms and damaging another 24 structures and 102 pipelines. In 2005, hurricanes Katrina and Rita destroyed or damaged 167 offshore platforms and 183 pipelines, shutting down production for weeks. Nineteen moveable drilling rigs snapped from their moorings and drifted, some as far as sixty miles. Six months later, 362,000 barrels of oil a day, out of a total previous production of one half million, remained shut off, along with 15% of the region's natural gas production (1.5 billion cubic feet per day). Repairing these structures is expensive and time-consuming. The Mars platform owned by Shell required $250-350 million to repair. Prior to Hurricane Katrina, Mars was producing about 140,000 barrels a day. It did not restart until late 2006, over a year after it was damaged.

Should future hurricane seasons bring further damage to production facilities in the Gulf of Mexico, it will raise the associated risks and undoubtedly, lead people to consider the relative merits of drilling in a colder climate — Alberta, and even northern Canada. As water temperatures in the Gulf of Mexico reach record levels, stronger hurricanes are forecast. Major oil and gas companies contemplating future investment will be inclined to add a risk and cost factor to any investments in the Gulf of Mexico. This may slow future oil and gas development in the Gulf of Mexico, and further squeeze production in that region.

It is also worth noting that according to the Energy Information Administration (EIA), many of the recently drilled gas wells in the Gulf have very high decline rates, which means that their life expectancy, even without hurricane damage, is not lengthy. The decline rate measures the drop in oil or gas production from a new well over time. Long-life wells might have a decline in annual production of 2-3%. Many of the wells being drilled currently, however, now have decline rates of 10%, 20%, and even 30%. These wells are only economic due to record prices. Their short life will compound the problem of future supply. As production declines, more new wells will be required. Eventually, as has already happened in the United States, decline in production cannot be offset by new drilling, and peak production occurs. Production declines, and demand mounts for imported oil and natural gas. Even President Bush, an oil man himself, conceded, "America is addicted to oil."

At the present time, Alberta produces two-thirds of Canada's oil and three-quarters of Canada's natural gas. From Alberta's revenue standpoint, the natural gas is more financially important, yielding $6.44 billion in royalties (2004-05) against $2 billion in oil royalties for the same period. By 2008, Alberta forecast over $11 billion in resource revenues. Of these revenues, over $5.1 billion will be from natural gas and $4.5 billion from oil.

The Alberta oil sands represent the greatest pool of unexploited oil within North America, and one of the largest remaining pools on the planet. With the oil sands included, only Saudi Arabia exceeds Canada in future oil reserves. This resource becomes additionally important because its proximity allows for the increasing transportation of oil by pipeline south into the United States and east into the industrial heartland of Canada. This importance is heightened by the fragility of supply from other parts of the world. The recent and dramatic increase in oil pricing has been a boon to the oil sands. Until now, the processes that allow extraction of oil from the sands involve the expenditure of a good deal of energy, usually natural gas. Other methods, however, are being developed and employed. Oil sand development requires an oil price in the $40-60-per-barrel range. At price levels above

$100 per barrel, hundreds of billions more dollars will be invested in the oil sands. This will sustain a strong economy, not just in Alberta, but throughout western Canada, with important revenue flows to other parts of the country. Alberta's oil sands could represent as much as 2.5 million barrels of oil per day for as long as 200 years.

Donald Coxe is a visionary who writes the Bank of Montreal's *Basic Points*, a monthly publication of evaluations and projections. Here is his lively take on the Alberta oil sands:

> We believe that the most readily available large-scale oil reserves in a politically secure area of the world are to be found in the Alberta oil sands. In discussions with experts, we have been led to believe that, depending on success of some experimental technologies, available reserves, assuming $40 oil, could be as high as 800 billion barrels – roughly four times the size Saudi reserves, which could substantially overstated.
>
> The Alberta Oil Sands are to the oil industry RLIs (Reserve Life Index) as Methuselah's lifespan is to human actuarial tables. An oil major that acquires a producing oil sands property gets an asset with a producing life that can do wondrous things for the major's RLI. It's rather as if a seventy-year-old male got injected with a Ponce de Leonesque chemical that could give the senior the life expectancy of a schoolboy. The market value of such a potion would be, one assumes, rather high.
>
> And so should the value of a producing oil sands property. However, under existing SEC rules, the value of an oil sands property in computing a company's RLI is indistinct, or even worthless. This means in the SEC's response to the industry's brief about using oil sands reserves in their corporate RLUs is a high-octane issue.
>
> We remain of the view that current SEC policy, drafted in the days of oil shale scams, should be updated in the light of those hundreds of billions of barrels of modern reality. Back then, OPEC had 15 million barrels a day

in excess pumping capacity. Today, that figure is one million – on a good day. The International Energy Agency's
Parisian boulevardiers have long earned tax-free incomes
to issue global oil supply and demand figures. Back then,
between glasses of premier grand cru wines, they agreed
with the most vocal latte liberals that the Chinese would
never be significant oil consumers because they loved
their bicycles too much. Back then, Big Oil was still a major weight in global stock indices, but its power and market capitalization had already entered long, seemingly
asymptomatic, decline.

For the SEC to uphold those oil reserve calculation
rules, issued a decade before the first barrel of Syncrude
light had gone to refinery, displays rather too much respect for the wisdom of the past. After all, we aren't talk-
ing of the Ten Commandments.

— *Basic Points*, Don Coxe, August 18, 2006

There are significant hurdles to the Alberta oil sands development. These challenges include severe shortages of construction workers and resulting inflation in housing costs
and wages. This may be beneficial to oil sector workers, but
has a distorting effect on wages in other sectors less able to
pay. That oil upgraders require vast quantities of water and
natural gas pose environmental and supply challenges. There
have been calls for a slowdown or even a moratorium in tar
sands development. Peter Lougheed, the former and well-regarded Premier of Alberta, suggested managed development
at a slower pace. Premier Stelmach may have slowed the pace
of development by his royalty decisions. Rising capital costs
may also slow development. New extraction methods may
reduce demands for water and natural gas. Nevertheless, the
large-scale development of oil extraction from the Alberta tar
sands over the next decade seems assured.

Investing in Energy

Investing in energy equities remains a cornerstone of my investment approach. We are burning through the planet's stock of oil and gas. Eventually, we will be forced to move to renewable forms of energy, such as wind, solar, and possibly hydrogen. For investors, "eventually" may not be that far away. In North America, the natural gas supply has not kept pace with demand. Prices have risen from $2 per McF to $5-14 per McF. More and more wells are being drilled, but the new wells have faster decline rates. A new well may lose 20% or 30% of its production after a year and be uneconomic after less than a decade. In some cases, wells are being drilled with life expectancies of less than five years. In the past, the standard life expectancy of wells exceeded ten years.

There are experts who forecast that the world oil supply will begin to decline somewhere between 2010 and 2020. Even President Bush is now campaigning to reduce U.S. oil dependence. Unfortunately, American tax incentives for the production of ethanol from corn have diverted a significant amount of food into fuel. Corn that previously fed the world now creates fuel for American cars. This has contributed to a sharp rise in world food prices. Food riots have been experienced in over thirty countries. Even if oil production continues to expand, it will do so at prices well above historic levels. These prices are likely to sustain the economics of Alberta oil sands development.

At present, there are two large clusters of relatively wealthy people on earth: some 300 million people in North America, and another 300 million in Europe, are relatively prosperous. What is less well-known is that amidst the nearly four billion people who live in Asia — mostly in India and China — are another 300 million people who are fast approaching European and North American income levels. This means there is explosive growth in demand in India and China for basic goods, such as housing and cars — both of which are major consumers of energy. As India and China move from being nations of bicycle riders to nations of car drivers, their oil consumption will increase rapidly.

Unending warfare in the Middle East does not help the stability of the oil supply, but the real factor here is the emergence of both China and India as major consumers of petroleum. As wealth increases in China and India, the emergent wealthy and middle-class populations are buying automobiles. Auto sales are growing 5-10% per month in China. Each new car brings new demand for gasoline. Over the past decade, annual consumption per person in China and India has been a mere one-half barrel, versus 45 barrels annual per capita in North America. What causes the difference? Cars!

Here is how Canada's Finance Department views our oil and gas reserve situation:

> The Rise of Emerging Economies Bodes Well for Canada's Resource Sector: Canada's rich natural resources and the industries they support are a vital part of our economy. This sector—forests, energy, minerals and metals, as well as related industries—accounts for 13 per cent of Canada's GDP, represents more than 40 per cent of Canadian exports and employs slightly more than 1 million Canadians. More recently energy consolidated its place as Canada's leading resource export sector. In 2004 energy exports reached a record $66 billion, driven by higher prices and new sources of supply. With rising oil prices in recent years, the share of energy in exports has more than doubled from 7.3 per cent in 1998 to 16.1 per cent in 2004.
>
> The Canadian resource sector is very capital-intensive, competitive and innovative. It is a diverse sector, well poised to benefit from a growing world need for alternative sources of energy, environmental technologies and the increasing interest in nuclear energy. Over the past decade, fully one-third of total investment in the Canadian economy has taken place in the natural re-

source sector, boosting gross capital stock by more than $400 billion since 1994. Over half of this expansion was in oil and gas, including megaprojects such as Hibernia, Terra Nova and Sable Island, and the Alberta oil sands. The non-conventional oil extraction industry, buoyed by prices that help the feasibility of many new projects, is the largest contributor to growth in the mining and oil and gas sector. The level of investment in the oil sands rose from $400 million in 1994 (or less than 4 per cent of investment in conventional projects) to $8.5 billion in 2005 (or 26 per cent of investment in conventional projects).

With its abundance and variety of natural resources, Canada is well positioned to take advantage of export opportunities arising from China and India's development and strong growth. Notably, Canada has a huge recoverable supply of crude oil and natural gas for future development. Crude oil reserves in 2002 were estimated at about 180 billion barrels, consisting of conventional oil (about 5 billion barrels) and oil sands (about 175 billion barrels). Today's annual oil production in Canada is about 940 million barrels, implying that the proven reserves could last almost 100 years even if the current rate of production were to double. Moreover, the ultimate recoverable potential from the Alberta oil sands is more than 315 billion barrels. The ultimate potential of Canadian natural gas supplies is estimated at nearly 600 trillion cubic feet, enough to last 100 years at current rates of production. (*Plan for Growth and Prosperity*, Department of Finance, Government of Canada, November 2005.)

One notes that the price of oil and natural gas affects how economic these resources are to extract.

Where to Invest in the Energy Sector?

All levels of the energy "food chain" offer opportunities. From giant multinational producers to energy trusts, from small exploration and production companies to energy services companies in drilling, there are plenty of good investment opportunities. The table below lists the larger energy companies.

Oil and Gas Fuels TSX

Oil and gas companies now comprise nearly 30% of the value of the TSX. Here are the top ten oil and gas companies by market capitalization in the TSX Forecast Index.

Company	Symbol	LS	Millions
Penn West Energy Trust	PWT.UN	30.53 -	11,425.18
Talisman Energy Inc	TLM	20.09 -	20,464.02
Petro-Canada	PCA	50.03	24,196.36
Husky Energy Inc	HSE	44.99	38,197.81
Nexen Inc	NXY	36.22	19,164.51
Canadian Natural Resources Ltd	CNQ	82.87	44,770.68
Suncor Energy Inc	SU	112	51,860.37
Imperial Oil Ltd	IMO	58.02	52,152.90
EnCana Corp	ECA	80.35	60,275.28
Canadian Oil Sands Trust	COS.UN	44.95	21,549.03

Opportunity in the Oil Sands

In 2006, Donald Coxe predicted in *Basic Points* that all current publicly traded oil sands companies will be acquired or taken private. Here are his four top candidates:

- Suncor Energy
- Western Oil Sands
- UTS Energy Corporation
- Canadian Oil Sands Trust

If Coxe is right, and he often is, then significant premiums — 15-35% — are likely to be paid to shareowners in the privatization process. If a bidding war for these properties emerged, premiums would be toward the higher end of the range. Will

Coxe be proven right? In mid-2007 Marathon Oil of Houston purchased Western Oil Sands for $6.5 billion CAD.

Opportunities Among Smaller Oil Sands Companies

OPTI Canada (OPC)

Symbol	Exchanges	Market Cap	Price (12 MoHigh)	Price (12 Mo Low)	Yield	P/E
OPC	T	$3.9 billion	$25.26	$15.30	-	n.a.

A small but interesting player in the oil sands is OPTI Canada. OPTI Canada is an oil sands company that concentrates on developing integrated oil sands projects in the Athabasca region of Alberta.

OPTI has working interests in three oil sands properties: Long Lake, Leismer and Cottonwood. It is developing a major project at Long Lake on a 50/50 basis with Nexen Inc.

Reasons to Buy:
- Oil sands player
- New technology for extraction (Integrated On Grade (TM) Process)
- On track for scheduled production in Q3 2008

Risks:
- Any production delays could negatively impact share price
- Commodity price decline for oil

(www.opticanada.com)

Petrobank Energy & Resources Ltd (PBG)

Symbol	Exchanges	Market Cap	Price (12 MoHigh)	Price (12 Mo Low)	Yield	P/E
PBG	T	$3.9 billion	$	$14.75	N/A	122

Petrobank Energy is a diversified oil company based in Calgary with conventional oil assets in Canada: the WHITE-SANDS oil project in Alberta, and 80.7% ownership of publicly-listed Petrominerales, which is one of the largest landholders exploring for oil in Colombia. Petrobank has a proprietary technology — THAI technology — which has the potential to improve recovery from the oil sands, with lower operating costs and lower carbon dioxide emissions. Petrobank's Heavy Oil Business Unit holds 62 sections of oil sands leases near Conklin, Alberta and is operating the WHITESANDS project to field-demonstrate their THAI heavy oil recovery process. In June 2007, Petrobank acquired the remaining interest in WHITESANDS Institute Ltd. As a result, Petrobank's interest in the WHITESANDS project increased from 84% to 100%.

I like Petrobank because of its three-pronged potential for continued value creation:

- Continued exploration of, and production growth from, its Bakken resource play in southeast Saskatchewan
- Resource expansion and production growth from its Colombian subsidiary, Petrominerales
- Resource expansion within its WHITESANDS oil project, and its continued development of THAI technology, which has the potential to improve the economic attractiveness of oil sands projects that meet the criteria

Reasons to Buy:

- Diversified portfolio of assets with great growth potential: North America and international (Latin America) — new technology for extraction
- Current production of 4,000bbl/d (Corcel-1) from the Putumayo Basin in Colombia, with eight more exploration wells planned in this area for 2008
- Overhaul of fiscal regime in 2004 in Colombia has resulted in lower royalty rates depending on volume (8% to 25%)
- Proprietary THAI technology being tested for greater bi-

tumen recovery in the oil sands — less energy intensive than the technologies in use
* Sizeable land position in the Athabasca Basin (28,800 acres) which an independent resource estimated to hold 2.6 billion barrels of bitumen

Risks:
* THAI process, which has never been used commercially, could falter and cause some downside risk to valuation
* Oil sands development is subject to regulatory approval (may be delayed due to high numbers of applications)
* Foreign risk in Colombia for Petrominerales, as there is no future guarantee of the country's political/economic situation

(www.petrobank.com)

Opportunities among Conventional Producers

There is a large array of energy companies from which to choose. You will also do well with most of the larger, well-regarded producers. Petro-Canada, Imperial Oil, and others, offer sustainable production from western Canada.

Opportunities Among Gas and Oil Trusts

My three favourite oil and gas trusts are Vermilion, Crescent Point, and Daylight Resources. The major difference between trusts and oil and gas producers organized as corporations is that trusts pay significant monthly distributions. This distribution of cash flow is valuable to investors as a means of participating in the income generated by the business.

Crescent Point Energy Trust (CPG.UN)

Symbol	Exchanges	Market Cap	Price (12 Mo High)	Price (12 Mo Low)	Yield	P/E
CPG.UN	T	$4.36	$34.60	$17.25	7.1%	

Crescent Point began its operations as an energy trust in September 2003. Its focus is on operating its own properties to produce light sweet crude oil. My particular interest is in the Bakken play where, in Q1 2008, Crescent Point drilled 52 wells with a 100% success rate. With an inventory of 1,400 low risk development locations, Crescent Point has enormous growth ahead of it. High oil prices will provide the cash flow and motivation to accelerate its Bakken drilling. With eight running drill rigs and current production of over 14,000 barrels of oil equivalent per day, Crescent Point is extremely well positioned.

Reasons to Buy:
• Six billion barrels of oil
• Huge number of potential wells to be drilled
• Saskatchewan environment favourable

Risks:
• Commodity price declines

(www.crescentpointenergy.com)

Daylight Resources Trust (Day.Un)

Symbol	Exchanges	Market Cap	Price (12 Mo High)	Price (12 Mo Low)	Yield	P/E
DAY.UN	T	$762 Million	$11.75	$6.06	12.3%	

Daylight Resources formed through the merger of Daylight Energy Trust and Sequoia Oil and Gas Trust in September 2006. Current production is 20,500 barrels of oil equivalent (BOE). At present, Daylight Resources is 60% natural gas but this is expected to shift to closer to 50/50 oil and gas over the next several years. A key asset is the trust's large land base — 680,000 areas in Alberta. Very strong formant agreements will likely replace 40% of Daylight Resources, current production with no capital outlay.

Reasons to buy:
- Sustainable payout ratio
- Yield of 12.3%
- Eight-year reserve life

Risks:
- Commodity price declines

Oil is Essential

Oil is a commodity that will propel the western Canadian economy over the medium and long-term. Canadian investors should be certain to own oil companies in their portfolios for the long-term.

3 The Benefit of Natural Gas – It's the Gas, Gas, Gas!

In February of 2006, TD Bank released a major commissioned report on natural gas entitled *Why Is It Always Oil? The Untold Story of Natural Gas*. The report captured headlines when it noted that natural gas is potentially more important to Canada than oil. Why? Simply put, gas has been worth more to Canada than oil.

Dubbing natural gas the "invisible commodity," the report advocates paying more attention to natural gas. The chief economist of the TD Bank, Derek Burleton, noted that in 2004, the value of Canadian natural gas production was 6.7% more than crude oil, a $2.5 billion difference. That same year, Canada exported $9.1 billion worth of crude oil more than it imported, while, natural gas net exports totalled $24.8 billion — almost three times the value of oil exports. Canada actually consumes about 70% of the crude oil that it produces, but less than half the domestic production of natural gas. The rest is exported. As noted earlier, natural gas has been a more important source of revenue than oil for producing provinces. That said, recent price increases for oil have been larger than for natural gas. Oil is closing this gap. As well, the increased oil production from Alberta oil sands is increasing the volume of Canada's oil production and also its total value.

Opportunity in Natural Gas – the Continental Clean Fuel

Why does oil command so much more public attention? Oil has the romantic advantage of travelling from exotic and dangerous parts of the world. But its profile may really arise from the visibility of paying at the gas pump, where motorists are continually reminded of oil price fluctuations. We focus more on the price of gasoline because it is a visible, frequent, out-of-pocket expense. Most Canadian homeowners who heat with natural gas pay their gas bill on a monthly basis, and most of us are on equalized monthly payment plans that smooth out the differences in winter and summer consumption. These factors may contribute to our dulled awareness. Whatever the reasons are for the misconception, the underlying economics dictate that natural gas be given more prominent consideration.

Natural gas, although hailing from the same ancient geology, is a vastly different economic proposition than oil. Oil travels better, or at least more readily, than gas. Oil tankers transport most of the world's oil across oceans. Natural gas is a largely continental fuel, because it is most readily transported by pipeline. As a gas, it needs to be transported in a compressed state. Pipelines are ideal for this. They transport large quantities long distances through compression provided by turbines stationed along the pipeline. Pipelines can be looped to gain more capacity. Greater quantities of gas can be moved by increasing compression through the addition of more pumping stations.

Consider these facts. First, natural gas production in the United States has been declining for many years despite the drilling of more and more wells. Second, almost all of the last 10,000 megawatts of electric generating capacity built in North

America was gas-fired, largely because of the better environmental impact of natural gas as a fuel. Third, due to its significant economic growth, Mexico, once an exporter of natural gas to the United States, has become an importer. Fourth, 77% of new dwellings in North America are built with central air conditioning. This is particularly true in the southern United States, where much recent home-building has occurred. This reality has shifted the demand for electricity from a single peak to double peaks: winter for heating and summer for cooling. This has significantly increased demand for electricity and for natural gas to fuel the generation of electricity.

Historically, natural gas has been injected into storage from April to October and drawn down from October to April. In July 2006, North America experienced its first ever summer drawdown of stored natural gas. Upon entering injection season in 2008, it was found that natural gas in storage is well below 2007 levels. Prices for natural gas have recently doubled.

In the Middle East and other parts of the world, there are enormous quantities of natural gas with no immediate local market. Already, industries that use significant quantities of gas, such as fertilizers and chemicals, have moved from North America to the Middle East. Gas can be transported across ocean in liquefied natural gas (LNG) carriers. These are vast spherical tanks that house gas under enormous pressure. Imports of LNG through existing LNG terminals are increasing, but there are two primary reasons that LNG is not likely to be a major solution to the natural gas demand situation in North America any time soon. Safety is the concern. Local residents are reluctant to allow LNG ports to be developed in their neighbourhood, and there is fear that LNG carriers could become a target for terrorists. The Government of New York recently vetoed a floating LNG port in Long Island Sound. While these concerns will likely slow the development of new LNG ports in North America, existing ports are likely to expand. Eventually, the natural gas on other continents will be needed for chemical feedstock, electric power generation and the heating of homes. As well, Asia and Europe will compete for available LNG supplies. There will be less natural gas than anticipated reaching American markets. As a result of these factors, Canadian natural gas is likely to command a bigger and bigger share of the U.S. market.

As noted, the major barrier to transporting natural gas in LNG carriers is community fear and the consequent local resistance to building LNG ports. There are two LNG ports in North America. One is five miles off Chesapeake Bay. The other is in an industrialized area of the Gulf of Mexico. It will likely be possible to build receptive gas ports in remote areas, although even on the remote coast of Maine, residents of Kennebunkport are putting up a determined struggle against the development of an LNG port in their backyard. It is unlikely that anyone will allow these carriers to enter major ports like Boston or New York due to citizen fears that one of these bulk carriers could be utilized to generate the equivalent of a nuclear explosion. It may turn out that LNG ports are built in remote locations and hooked up to existing pipeline capacity.

For an investor, the major point is that new LNG capacity will not occur quickly. It will be at least five or six years before any incremental LNG capacity can transport much gas into North America. We've already seen the price of natural gas move from a historic range of $2-4 per McF up to $5-10 per McF. Korea paid $20 per McF for LNG in 2008. Most forecasters see the price of natural gas increasing over the medium and longer-term. There has been some demand reduction, as chemical industries, which use natural gas as feedstock for fertilizer and plastics, have moved plants to parts of the world where gas supplies are cheaper. For those interested in petrochemicals, the most likely future realignment will be the construction of a global petrochemical industry in the Middle East, in countries like the United Arab Emirates which are based around a very large supply of natural gas. Currently, much of that gas is flared — burnt in the atmosphere

— causing both pollution and loss of economic value. From an investment point of view, oil is a world commodity readily transported in tankers, and therefore, a commodity that trades on the last barrel. Natural gas, not so readily moved, can have vastly different prices in different parts of the world. It could be very cheap in the Middle East and very expensive in Europe and North America. As noted, more LNG plants and vessels will be built, but this will take considerable time. It's more likely that petrochemical plants, fertilizer plants and other major gas users will continue to move to gas-rich parts of the world.

The North American natural gas supply situation is another story of diminishing returns. The major easy-to-access fields in North America have long since been tapped, though not exhausted. What is underway now is the use of much improved seismic, including three-dimensional seismic, to locate new, generally smaller, deposits. Seismic is the use of sound waves to locate potential oil and gas deposits. A variety of new and improved drilling techniques, including horizontal drilling, are being utilized to tap into these gas deposits. The other reality for North American gas, particularly in the Western Canadian Sedimentary Basin where there's a good deal of infrastructure to transport it, is that the quadrupling price has made much smaller reserves much more economical. Some gas wells that were drilled and abandoned in the 1950s and 1960s are being reopened. With gas peaking at $10-15 per McF, these wells are now proving not just economical, but very profitable for the small operators who are engaging in these re-drilling enterprises. These smaller, shallower reserves, however, have higher decline rates and as such, short life expectancies.

Canada offers a rich array of ways for investors to participate in natural gas. For the cautious, there are very high quality gas utilities that transport gas across the country and south into the American market, and there are pipelines that deliver gas to people's homes. There are also infrastructure pipeline and related facility trusts such as Keyera, Fort Chicago, Pembina Pipeline and Inter Pipe. These trusts pay investors a significant monthly return on their investment. Growth in their infrastructure for natural gas transportation and processing also builds investor value. These trusts are covered in Chapter 7 as part of a review of utilities. This chapter is about the opportunities to invest more directly in companies producing natural gas.

Opportunities Among Gas Producers

There are several major producers, the most prominent and interesting of which is EnCana. During his term as CEO, Gwyn Morgan took a very different road with EnCana. He sold off EnCana's international assets and consolidated into unconventional gas, in which EnCana has unique and deep expertise. Unconventional gas is the extraction of gas from "tight sands," that is, sands that are not very porous. Disavowing conventional wisdom, Morgan took the company out of the North Sea and the global markets, and focused on western Canada and, increasingly, the U.S. Rockies. His sole focus became tight gas plays. EnCana is now a huge company with a market cap over the $60 billion range. EnCana is a top choice for those who share my view that natural gas in Canada will be an invaluable asset over the next decade. You'll want to buy EnCana in the "shoulder" season, that is, in the spring or fall when its price declines with the annual fluctuations in the price of natural gas.

EnCana (ECA) *Nov. 20/09*

Symbol	Exchanges	Market Cap	Price (12 Mo High)	Price (12 Mo Low)	Yield	P/E
ECA	T-NY	$62 billion	$88.06	$57.61	1.98	17.3

EnCana Corporation is a major natural gas producer in North America, where it holds natural gas and oil resource lands.

Recently, it became the most valuable company on the Toronto Stock Exchange.

Reasons to Buy:
- Pure natural gas company and largest Canadian company by value
- Worldwide, the best operator of tight sands gas
- Expanding coal bed methane production in Western Basin
- Largest player in promising Montney, B.C. play — the Montney play is an area of rich oil-baring sands

Risks:
- Gas price declines are possible
- Provincial royalty increases recently announced by Premier Stelmach will negatively affect EnCana
- Future competition from LNG shipments

(www.encana.com)

Other major producers of natural gas in Canada include Talisman Energy (TLM), Canadian Natural Resources (CNQ), and Nexen (NXY). All are worthy of serious investment consideration. Talisman Energy has a large exposure to natural gas, although in recent years, its stock market track record has been mediocre.

Trusts and Gas

The second way to invest in natural gas is to get to the intermediate producers and some of the gassier of the energy royalty trusts.

Vermilion Energy Trust (VET.UN)

Symbol	Exchanges	Market Cap	Price (12 Mo High)	Price (12 Mo Low)	Yield	P/E
VET.UN	T	2.7 Billion	$40.40	$31.00	5.51%	

The Benefit of Natural Gas

Vermilion Energy Trust was established under an arrangement with Vermilion, Vermilion Resources Ltd., Clear Energy Inc & Vermilion Acquisition Ltd. The company's main order of business is developing oil and natural gas resources through acquisition and production. These operations are located, for the most part, in Canada, France, the Netherlands and Australia. Vermilion also has a major stake in Verenex Energy, which is currently drilling successful oil wells in Libya. Verenex could be a source of considerable value to Vermilion.

Reasons to Buy:
- Diverse international asset base
- Natural gas produced in Europe as well as Canada
- Top pick in energy trust sector
- 35.3% annual rate of return over five years, including distribute reinvestment
- Verenex upside

Risks:
- Commodity price declines
- Political risk in Libya

(*www.vermillionenergy.com*)

In my view, the natural gas play in North America is not a phenomenon of a few weeks, months or even years. This is a profound and permanent shift in the value of this once poorly-regarded commodity. The cleanliness and versatility of natural gas has transformed it into an enormously valuable commodity, with benefits for all involved. Despite low prices in 2007 and early 2008, both the medium and longer term promise to reward patient investors. Several other trusts with high exposure to natural gas are listed below:

Trusts with Significant Natural Gas Exposure

Paramount Energy	100%
Progress Energy	85%
Enerplus Resource Fund	60%
Advantage Energy Income Fund	64%
Peyto Energy	82%
Trilogy Energy	79%

** Focus Trust merged with Enerplus in Feburary 2008.
Source: Corporate Annual Reports

Investing in Explorecos

Finally, for the more courageous, there are small exploration companies, known as explorecos. These companies have the capacity to grow rapidly — but they can, just as quickly, lose value in the marketplace based on a single failed play, or in some cases, an expensive well. Investors would be best advised to buy a small cluster of the smaller producers and diversify exposure. Any single firm could represent substantial risk if its drilling comes up dry. It is also likely that some of these small producers will grow their production into the intermediate range. Lately, some of them have either been acquired or converted into income trusts, as with True Energy. The following explorecos have a strong focus on the natural gas side.

#3.93   52wH #6.32

Vero Energy Inc. (VRO) *Nov. 2/09   L #2.70*

Symbol	Exchanges	Market Cap	Price (12 Mo High)	Price (12 Mo Low)	Yield	P/E
VRO	T	$238 million	$11.34	$5.36	0%	9.9

Vero Energy is an exploreco in Alberta. It explores, develops and produces natural gas and crude oil. The company commenced oil and gas operations in November 2005 after the closing of a plan of arrangement between Vero, True Energy, and TKE Energy Trust. On November 2,

2005, certain oil and gas properties of True Energy were transferred to Vero. This was a spinout of assets from the trust. On February 24, 2006, Vero acquired all of the issued and outstanding shares of Ledge Resources Limited, a private Alberta oil and gas exploration and development company. On January 1, 2007, Vero and its wholly owned subsidiaries were amalgamated under the name Vero Energy Inc. The company entered 2007 with production of 5,700 BOE which represents a 46% increase over the 2006 exit production rate. Additionally, Vero has increased its proved and probable reserves by 64% over its 2007 level.

Reasons to Buy:
- Excellent exploration track record
- Efficient developer of new production

Risks:
- Commodity prices declines

(*www.veroenergy.com*)

Storm Exploration Inc. (SEO) *Nov. 20/09*

Symbol	Exchanges	Market Cap	Price (12 Mo High)	Price (12 Mo Low)	Yield	P/E
SEO	T	$802 million	$19.75	$7.27	0%	

Storm Exploration Inc is a Calgary-based junior oil and gas company engaged in the exploration, acquisition, development and production of oil and natural gas reserves in Alberta and British Columbia.

Storm has 229,000 net acres of undeveloped land base spanning northeast British Columbia, as well as the Grande Prairie, Red Earth and Surmont regions in Alberta. The company's 2008 focus is on the Parkland area in northeast B.C., targeting the Doig, Halfway and Montney natural gas zones. The Parkland and Grande Prairie areas have contributed the majority of current production (over 6,000 BOE per day), but given the shift in Storm's focus, the Parkland is expected to account for most of the forward growth in production. Storm expects to produce an average of 8,000 BOE per day in 2008, up from 6,800 BOE per day in 2007. The Storm management team has built two previous companies and successfully sold for a premium to larger players, therefore it is experienced at operating at much lower natural gas and oil prices. This discipline shows up in the company's low operating costs ($7.07 per BOE in 2007) and total cash costs ($9.98 per BOE in 2007), which means, at current gas and oil prices, Storm is producing very strong cash flows.

Reasons to Buy:
- Montney opportunity for new gas production
- Gas focused
- Successful drilling program

Risks:
- Commodity price declines

(www.stormexploration.com)

Highpine Oil & Gas Ltd (HPX)

Handwritten: ↑7.57 Nov. 20/09   52W H ↑7.62   L ↓3.7

Symbol	Exchanges	Market Cap	Price (12 Mo High)	Price (12 Mo Low)	Yield	P/E
HPX	T	Million	$	$	%	

Highpine Oil & Gas Limited is a Canada-based oil and gas company. Highpine is engaged in exploration, development, and production of crude oil, natural gas and natural gas liquids in western Canada. Substantially, all of Highpine's exploration and development activities are conducted jointly with others. In February 2006, it acquired White Fire Energy Ltd, and in August 2006, Kick Energy Corporation. Kick was an oil and natural gas exploration and production company active in the Western Canadian Sedimentary Basin. In 2007, the company produced 17,655 of BOE, representing a nearly 50% increase over 2006 production.

Reasons to Buy:
- Increasing production
- Expanded capital program

Risks:
- Commodity price declines
- Higher royalty rates

(www.highpine.com)

The Gas Benefit

From an investor's standpoint, investing in natural gas in the ground in western Canada is one of the soundest possible medium and long-term investments. This is not to suggest investors suspend the normal rules of stock selection. Rather, in a broad sense, natural gas dramatically increased in value, and the companies that find, drill, and deliver it to the market all stand to benefit from this value increase.

4 Oil and Gas Services Companies

Oil and gas do not leap out of the ground unassisted. Extracting oil and gas from deep underground is a complex, scientific business. Companies within the services industry do everything from drilling to supplying camps for workers. My affection is great for investing in companies and trusts in the oil and gas services business over the long-term. Drilling and myriad other services supplied by these companies will be profitable businesses as long as they are prudently managed, regardless of whether oil remains at $120, soars to $200 or sags below $70. Why? Simply put, pools of oil and gas in the Western Canadian Sedimentary Basin are getting harder and harder to find. This means that all sorts of new techniques, such as horizontal drilling, are in demand to fund and extract resources.

A May 2006 study conducted by the Canadian Gas Potential Committee underscores this reality. The study notes that the large, easy-to-access pools of gas have already been discovered. They estimate that to date, in western Canada, we've "discovered 70% of the resource (natural gas) in 40,000 pools. The remaining 30% of natural gas is going to be discovered in 440,000 pools."

Consider the implications of this statement. Discovering and producing the remaining 30% will require tapping 11 times more pools than the first 70%. The effort will increase by nearly twenty-five-fold. This is tough news for oil and gas exploration companies, but a bonanza for drillers and the oil and gas services industry. Higher prices will make smaller pools more economical and viable, but much more work will be required to extract the product. This will translate into thousands of jobs, higher production costs, and exponential growth in this sector.

The ramp up in the drilling of natural gas wells is to invest in one of the drilling companies. Precision Drilling, Ensign (now a trust), Akita Drilling and Savanna, are all examples of these companies. Drilling companies make their money on the volume of wells drilled and the price paid per well. Strongly in their favour is not only that more wells are being drilled but that the wells are, in most cases, being drilled to deeper depths. As a consequence, the cost per well has been rising. The drilling companies are the chief beneficiaries of the diminishing returns in the Western Canadian Sedimentary Basin as they have to drill more and more to find less and less gas. The risk for drilling companies is a slowdown in drilling which would be triggered by a slowdown or a drop in the price of natural gas. A sharp increase in cost of land could also slow the pace of drilling.

Beyond the drillers, there are other companies involved in the oil services industry. Some have converted to income trusts, such as Wellco and Eveready, but others, like Finning and Calfrac, benefit from increased activity in the oil patch. All of these companies were also clobbered by the slowing of activity in 2007, but are rebounding in 2008. The medium term will prove more buoyant for their volumes of business and for investors.

Akita Drilling

My favourite driller, Akita Drilling, is controlled by the Southern family of Calgary. Ron Southern is better known for his investment in ATCO, and best known for manufacturing trailers seen on construction sites worldwide. I have owned shares in Akita Drilling for ten years. From a price of $4, it now trades in the $14-20 range, after a two-for-one share split.

Going along for the ride in companies with controlling shareholders is not always a great investment strategy. However, in companies with exceptional owners, it can be very profitable. Fortunately, Akita has been one of those companies with an excellent owner, and is generous to minority shareholders.

It has become popular in corporate governance circles to denounce corporations where a single shareholder or family exerts dominant control. Certainly, there have been structural abuses — multiple voting shares — in Canadian corporate governance. And there are a few horror stories, such as Hollinger and Conrad Black. However, it doesn't stand to reason that a company with a dominant owner will do worse for its shareholders than one wherein ownership is broadly distributed. It all depends on the quality of ownership and the determination to create value, either narrowly, for the company itself, or more broadly, for all shareholders.

Akita Drilling is a modest-sized but highly successful oil and gas drilling company based in Calgary. The Southern family have become very wealthy through their ownership of ATCO and Canadian Utilities. Ron Southern is the entrepreneur who serves as Chair of the Board of ATCO and Canadian Utilities, as well as Akita Drilling. His family controls roughly 86% of the voting shares of Akita Drilling through Class B shares. The Class A shares, which are owned by the public, do not have the right to vote in normal circumstances. Ron Southern, who, by owning 86.2% of the Class B common shares, controls the corporation, also owns 22.9% of the Class A shares.

Oil and Gas Services Companies

When I began my investment management career at Lawrence Decter Investment Counsel, I was pleased to meet with a succession of oil and gas analysts, some of whom wrote research reports in the oil services sector. They always presented research on much larger companies, such as Precision Drilling and Ensign Resources. Whenever I inquired as to whether or not they covered Akita Drilling, they would always say no. Sometimes, they were honest enough to say that the reason they did not cover Akita Drilling was because it had a dominant shareholder. Indeed, Akita Drilling's board of directors also includes Ron's wife, Margaret, and their daughter Nancy — who has also served as president of ATCO and Canadian Utilities. This is a very large family business. Based on the surface facts, many would caution against such an investment. It would certainly raise the hackles of the good corporate governance crowd. The Southern family has three members on the board of directors and an absolute lock on control of Akita through their ownership of the voting shares. But let's consider the performance of the company as an investment, on the basis that no investment will perform very well unless the underlying company is successful.

A careful review of Akita Drilling's annual reports reveals the growth of the company. In 1994, Akita Drilling had just over $60 million in revenue. It had net earnings of $7 million and earnings per share of $0.77. Shareholders' equity per share was $3.03. Over ten years, revenue more than doubled to $124 million in 2003. By 2006, revenue was $174 million. Earning per share rose from $0.68 to 1998 to $1.83 in 2006. Shareholders' equity per share more than tripled from $3.03 to $9.43. While there was some volatility in the earnings through the ups and downs of the oil and gas price cycle, growth in shareholders' equity per share was steady through the period. In fact, there was no year in which shareholder equity did not grow. Even in 2007, when revenue and earnings dipped, shareholders' equity increased to $10.29. This is strong evidence of a well-managed company. Akita has also maintained a conservative balance sheet. Akita has taken additional debt only to build drill rigs that were contracted on a multi-year base through joint ventures to clients. This contracting ensures that the debt will be retrieved from dependable revenues.

The company has performed extremely well over the period of a decade. In mid-2004, shares of Akita Drilling traded in the range of $25 and $26. Following a two-for-one stock split, the shares resumed their climb and are trading in the $14-20 range, after touching $24. Clearly, this has been an outstanding investment for patient shareholders.

In addition to appreciation on the price of the shares, Akita began paying dividends to its shareholders in 1996. In 1999, it paid $0.28 per share; in 2000, $0.32; in 2001, $0.36; in 2003, $0.36; in 2004, $0.40; and in 2006, after a two-for-one share split, the dividend was $0.24 cents. In 2007, it increased to $0.28 — the equivalent of $0.56 before the share split. This sustained track record indicates a willingness to enhance shareholder value.

Additional steps taken to improve share price value for shareholders include what are called Normal-Course Issuer Bids (NCIBs). In this process, the company uses some of its cash flow to buy back shares in the market, thereby reducing the number of total outstanding shares and increasing value per share for remaining shareholders. In 2003, Akita repurchased over 140,500 Class A non-voting shares — about 1.7% of the total class — at an average price of $21.31 per share. By the end of 2005, all long-term debt had been paid off. In 2005 and 2006, an additional 69,100 shares were repurchased.

Furthermore, these dominant owners of the company do not appear to take any excessive payments by way of directors' fees. An annual retainer of $14,000 per member of the board and $1,000 per meeting is paid to directors. This is modest when compared to the standards of other Canadian companies. Nor is there evidence of extreme executive pay. Over the last three years, the CEO has received an annual salary of

$350,000; two of the yearly bonuses awarded were $350,000, and last year, it was $105,000.

In addressing the standard questions on governance, the Akita Information Circular notes the following:

> The Corporation is controlled by Mr. Ron Southern and Mr. Southern is therefore significant shareholder within the meaning of the guidelines. Eight of the directors have relationships with the significant shareholder as contemplated in the guidelines. Although the board considers independence from significant shareholders a factor in assessing the qualification of potential candidates, the board's primary objective is to ensure the directors are the most qualified candidates available and are selected on the basis of their overall qualifications and their abilities to contribute to the effective governance of the corporation. All of the corporation directors make a valuable contribution to the board, the corporation and shareholders. The directors are at all times mindful of the interests of the minority shareholders.

While this statement might seem self-serving, it must be juxtaposed against the obvious reality of Akita's performance. As a minority shareholder, I'm delighted to be along for the ride with the Southern family, and have enjoyed the enormous success of the corporation as a shareholder, and as an investment manager who has purchased shares of Akita for my clients.

While as many oil and gas service companies become over-extended in boom years, Akita's conservative approach to its balance sheet and its effort to enter into joint ventures with long-term arrangements make it a particularly appealing company. Between 2000 and 2001, Akita entered into long-term contracts with large corporations and constructed five drilling rigs. These long-term contracts guarantee work for the drill rig once constructed, and greatly lesson the risk of a downturn in overall activity impacting the company balance sheet. Akita has also pursued new opportunities in methods of drilling and, of late, has focused on drilling for coal bed methane (CBM), which may be the next large opportunity for growth in drilling. CBM is the next wave of natural gas exploration and production. As early as 2003, Akita drilled 101, or one-third, of the CBM wells. This has made Akita a pioneer in this new drilling segment, a position that is serving it well as CBM drilling expands.

Akita Drilling Ltd (AKT.A) *Nov. 20/09*

+9.42   52wH ↑12.44   L ↑5.25

Symbol	Exchanges	Market Cap	Price (12 Mo High)	Price (12 Mo Low)	Yield	P/E
AKT.A	T	$241 million	$18.90	$9.51	1.93 %	13.69

Akita Drilling is an oil and gas drilling and well servicing contractor with operations throughout western Canada, Canada's northern territories and Alaska. In addition to conventional drilling and well services, the company specializes in purpose-built Arctic and heavy oil drilling, providing specialized drilling services to a broad range of independent and multinational oil and gas companies. Akita employs approximately 800 people and operates 37 drilling rigs in all depth ranges.

Reasons to Buy:
- Well-positioned for resumption of drilling in the Mackenzie Valley
- Solid balance sheet with little debt
- Able to maintain profitability in oil patch downturns

Risks:
- Delays in Mackenzie Valley Pipeline
- Cyclical downturn in oil and gas services sector

(*www.akita-drilling.com*)

Savanna Energy Services

Savanna is another unique opportunity to invest in the drilling of the western oil and gas patch. Founded in 2001, Savanna had become a strong performer prior to its merger with Western Lakota. Realizing that First Nations citizens are an increasingly important element of the oil business, Western Lakota partnered with First Nations people to build oil drilling rigs and place them into service on a partnership basis. Western Lakota benefitted from the revenue from constructing rigs, and also, the operating revenue once they are in service.

From a standing start in 2001, Western Lakota had achieved revenues of $105 million in 2005 prior to the merger, with Savanna and that year, net income exceeded $21 million. Rapid growth through partnerships and partnership financing has characterized the growth of the company.

The business model adopted by Western Lakota and continued by Savanna should serve it well as drilling moves north into territories with First Nations and Inuit involvement. Partnerships, including substantial share ownership by the Métis and Samson Cree Nations, have opened the door to many Aboriginal arrangements. Chief Victor Buffalo serves on the Savanna Energy Services Board.

Savanna Energy Services Corp (SVY) *Nov. 20/09*

Symbol	Exchanges	Market Cap	Price (12 Mo High)	Price (12 Mo Low)	Yield	P/E
SVY	T	$1.2 billion	$23.49	$13.13	0.47%	22.5

Savanna provides a variety of services in the oil and natural gas industry. It primarily operates through three main operating companies, all of which are 100% owned subsidiaries of Savanna. The company segments include corporate, service rigs and drilling. The corporate segment provides management and administrative services to all its subsidiaries and their respective operations; the service rig segment provides well servicing to the oil and gas industry; the drilling segment provides primarily contract drilling services to the oil and gas industry through both conventional and hybrid drilling rigs. In 2006, the well servicing division operated an average of 22 service rigs, six coil service trucks and 12 boilers.

Reasons to Buy:
- Second highest market share in the drilling market in the Western Canadian Sedimentary Basin
- Rise in oil prices to all-time high of $93, causing greater company margins
- Shortage of drilling rigs in the oil sector gives Savanna greater pricing power
- Great flexibility on its balance sheet to pursue strategic acquisitions, as well as grow organically through its proprietary hybrid drilling technology

Risks:
- Lower oil and natural gas prices
- Royalty increase in western Canada, specifically Alberta, causing slowdown in drilling demand

(*www.savannaenergy.com*)

Pipeline Income Trusts

A fairly conservative way of participating in the growth of the Alberta oil business is through pipeline trusts. These trusts offer decent returns with little business risk. These are discussed in detail in Chapter 9: The Utility of Utilities, as a particular type of utility income trust.

Energy Savings Income Fund
Rebecca MacDonald is the dynamic founder of Energy Savings Income Fund. An award-winning entrepreneur, MacDonald came to Canada from her native Hungary trained

as a physician. In the weird and sometimes perverse system that Canada utilizes to license graduates of foreign medical schools, Dr. MacDonald was denied permission to practice. Undeterred by this, she set about to build a business enterprise and succeeded in a dynamic and fascinating fashion. Her new business was selling natural gas one household at a time.

Curious. And you thought utilities themselves sold natural gas and electricity to customers, such as individuals and businesses. This was true until the deregulation of natural gas and, in some parts of North America, electricity. MacDonald realized the opportunity that existed to give retail customers, that is, homeowners and small businesses, a fixed price, so these customers wouldn't have to face the volatility and potential increase of commodity prices. Legend has it, that originally, MacDonald sold contracts door-to-door. Now, she heads an organization that has an overall market value into the hundreds of millions of dollars and provides a service to nearly a million customers. The essence of her business is to buy gas over a multi-year period — five years — and market it to retail customers. In essence, Energy Savings Income Fund serves as a distributor of natural gas and, more recently, electricity. The company's strategy is to purchase matching volumes of gas and electricity; they thereby eliminate customer exposure to price escalations. The fund logs in its margins by entering into long-term fixed-price contracts.

In addition to continually adding new long-term customers, the second part of MacDonald's genius has been to keep investors happy by steady but small increases in the distributions. In 2007, Energy Savings also announced a distribution increase. This increase was to $1.065 per unit, effective 2008. The gradual increase in distributions has been an important feature of the fund. It clearly establishes that the fund is interested in growth, both geographically, and in terms of commodities and customers. That growth is evident in the steady financial progress of the company.

Energy Savings is definitely one of the good trusts. It rewards its initial investors with an excellent return. Measured from the go-public-date to the present, the return has been exceptional. Since going public in April 2001 at $10 per unit, the units have returned over 46.5% to investors (as of September 2007). At its peak in September 2005, the company's units traded for $21.52, representing a return of 115.2%. This trust remains an outstanding performer over the long-term. Now the units trade at $13.89 per unit. This reflects investor skepticism about future growth rates being sustained.

Energy Savings Income Fund (SIF.UN)

Symbol	Exchanges	Market Cap	Price (12 Mo High)	Price (12 Mo Low)	Yield	P/E
SIF.UN	T	$1.4 billion	$17.66	$12.29	13.93	11.7

Energy Savings Income Fund is an open-ended trust that owns and distributes the income from several wholly-owned subsidiaries and affiliates: Ontario Energy Savings L.P., Energy Savings (Manitoba) Corp, Energy Savings (Quebec) L.P., ES (B.C.) Limited Partnership, Alberta Energy Savings L.P., Illinois Energy Savings Corp, New York Energy Savings Corp and Indiana Energy Savings Corp. Energy Services sells natural gas to residential and small to mid-size commercial customers under long-term, fixed-price contracts. In Ontario, Alberta and New York, Energy Savings also supplies electricity to customers under fixed-price contracts.

Reasons to Buy:
- High yield
- Continued customer growth in Canada and the U.S.; U.S. customer base increased 42% in 2007
- Expansion in New York State and Indiana
- Very high return on capital
- Future entry into B.C. residential market

Risks:
- Lower natural gas prices
- Slower customer growth
- Smaller gross margins
- Margin pressure in U.S. market

(www.energysavings.com)

Opportunities for Investors

Canada's oil, gas and related service companies and trusts offer terrific opportunities for Canadian investors. A word of advice on timing: despite the overall long-term upward trend in energy prices, there are still cyclical and seasonal ups and downs. You are best to buy when others are gloomy. Late summer, when storage is filled by injecting natural gas in anticipation of winter, usually features low natural gas prices and good buying opportunity. Buy drillers when they are beaten up, their store prices are low, and their prospects for future business are growing. By the pipeline trusts anytime – they are steady income earnings.

5 Peace, Order and Government Healthcare

In the 1970s, when I was working for the Cabinet Office of the Manitoba government, one of my colleagues, a talented architect and land use planner, David Johns, built a magnificent house thirty kilometres northeast of Winnipeg, beside Birds Hill Provincial Park. His neighbour was an elderly farmer who raised garlic on a small acreage and had not been to Winnipeg in sixty years. David asked his neighbour whether or not he preferred Canada to the part of Europe he had left in the early 20th century to escape World War I. "Yes, I like it here better," the farmer replied. "No wars." Although it's a simple, perhaps even simplistic, statement, it has the virtue of truth.

The last war on Canadian soil was the War of 1812, wherein we defeated the Americans. Since Canada did not exist as a nation until 1867, it would be more accurate to say that British Canada, or even the British, defeated the Americans. To maintain the American view of us as their peaceable northern neighbours, we will skip lightly over the 1812 torching of the White House. For nearly 200 years, no wars have been fought on Canadian soil. No terrorists have succeeded in attacking Canada, although arrests would suggest that terrorist acts have been planned. No Canadian prime minister has ever been assassinated. In fact, one of our recent prime ministers, Jean Chrétien, gained notoriety for attempting to strangle a protestor. In Canada, citizens may be marginally more at risk from our leaders than vice versa! Peace, therefore, is a much valued facet of our country — so valued, that most days, we take it for granted.

Canada has a strong historical claim to make on the international peace front. We have contributed more than our share to United Nations' peacekeeping efforts. Prime Minister Lester B. Pearson received the 1957 Nobel Peace Prize for his efforts in this regard. "Peace, order, and good government" comprise the trinity of principles embedded in Canada's constitutional history, in contrast to the more aggressive "life, liberty and the pursuit of happiness" creed that is central to America's Declaration of Independence. Canadians find they are comfortable with the more pedestrian "peace, order and good government," that underlies our constitution.

What does this have to do with Canada as place to invest? Canada's relationship to peace creates four elements that are key to lucrative investment. First, we don't have the massive expense of a vast military patrol of the world. Second, we are well-regarded among the nations of the world as a peace-seeking and peacemaking nation, which renders us less likely to be attacked by others. Third, we didn't colonize other nations, outside our borders, so there's no legacy of external empire to contend with in our future. Fourth, we have, under our belt, several hundred years of negotiating our nation's future without significant internal violence. These realities make Canada an attractive place to live and invest.

Canada may also be one of the most successful multicultural and multiracial nations. Through its policy of accepting refugees and immigrants from all corners of the world, Canada has developed ethnically diverse cities, particularly in Toronto, Montreal and Vancouver. Granted, immigrants often experience difficulties in finding employment, and our education system has struggled to provide sufficient English as a Second Language programs. As a nation built upon waves of immigration, however, Canada has not experienced the integration difficulties of European countries with more unitary populations — most notably France, but also in the Scandinavian nations and the Netherlands. There have been no violent uprisings by disaffected immigrants. Our earlier history is less compelling but our present policy stance seems to be working. Peace is good for investors because violence erodes consumer confidence.

Order has also been a Canadian virtue. This relatively peaceful country of ours is evident in the following table contrasting the number of homicides per year in Canada versus other countries. Canada remains a peaceful northern neighbour to the United States which, with its constitutional right to bear arms, is a strikingly more dangerous place to live. Canada is comparable to the United Kingdom and Australia. Canada is only significantly more dangerous than Japan, and is vastly safer than Russia. Order is good for investors, who need not fear that violence will increase social loss and uncertainty.

Homicides (1998 to 2000)

Country	Total Per Year	Per 100,000 Population
Canada	489	1.49
United States	12,658	4.28
United Kingdom	850	1.41
Russia	28,904	20.01
Australia	302	1.50
Netherlands	183	1.11
Japan	637	0.49
India	37,170	3.44

Seventh United Nations Survey of Crime Trends and Operations of Criminal Justice Systems, 1998 – 2000 (United Nations Office of Drug and Crime, Centre for International Crime Prevention)

Peace, Order and Government Healthcare

A violent society is an expensive society. According to *The Washington Post*, the United States spends an estimated $60 billion each year to house more than two million inmates in prisons and jails. Canada, by contrast, has only 35,000 prison inmates — less than 2% of the U.S. total. The cost is not only the cost of incarceration — it is also the tens of billions of dollars of lost productivity to the economy.

For most of our history, Canada has enjoyed an enviable reputation for good government. In recent years, a series of government scandals has called our enviable record into question. At a national level, the scandals — notably the Sponsorship Scandal, investigated by Justice John H. Gomery — decimated the fortunes of a governing federal Liberal Party in the province of Quebec. There has also been a major scandal in Toronto's City Hall, and several provincial governments have had minor scandals of their own. Still, on a relative basis, Canada enjoys honest government and government officials, although a case could be made that Canada has too much government. The combination of governments at provincial and federal levels is onerous. This is the burden of the confederation. The unending tug of war on the provincial and federal levels over resources and jurisdiction can be wearing, but often, these conflicts are resolved in creative ways to the benefit of the province concerned, and of the nation.

The debate over Quebec's role in Canada and the emergence of a strong separatist movement has led to periodic upheaval and anxiety. With the exception of a brief period — the War Measures Act, nearly forty years ago — all of this advocacy has been conducted peacefully. As well, constitutional negotiations, properly dubbed the unending trip to the dentist, have fatigued our body politic on a recurring basis. Despite this, the Canadian nation and its Constitution and *Charter of Rights and Freedoms* work well in practice.

Government Healthcare

Medicare in Canada is generally known as our most prized social program. Canadian medicare is our universal, comprehensive, battered and bruised, yet unbowed, system of public healthcare insurance. In fact, in 2004, its champion, Tommy Douglas, was voted Greatest Canadian in CBC's national television search, because of his achievement of medicare. In Canadian politics, to be seen as against medicare can be career-ending. And yet, little attention is focused on the benefit to business of our comprehensive public insurance scheme. To be fair, business and individuals do bear some of the cost for healthcare in Canada. The cost of insuring health services in Canada is split on a roughly 70-30 basis, with the majority of the costs — 70% — paid by the government with revenues collected through the tax system and through various levees or premiums. This 70% covers virtually all hospital and doctor services, as well as the majority of homecare and long-term care services. The drug bill is split, with the government picking up a little better than a third of the total cost. The 30% paid by employers and individuals goes largely to dental costs for employees, drug plan costs, supplementary health benefits such as private hospital rooms, and cost-sharing by patients. This 30% also includes supplementary insurance purchased by Canadians to cover health costs while travelling, and other gaps in the public system. Medicare's broad shoulders support the costs of health services in Canada, rather than dumping the majority of costs on employers and individuals.

There is one major unfinished aspect of the coverage medicare is intended to provide Canadians — comprehensive coverage for medications. As in other industrialized nations, Canada has experienced a rapid rise in drug spending. Last year alone, according to the Canadian Institute for Health, drug spending rose 11% to $24 billion. Unlike hospital and physician care, which are overwhelmingly covered by public insurance, coverage for medications is a patchwork quilt, something like the mixed approach of the United States to health insurance in general. In Canadian hospitals, drug costs are covered by public insurance. Outside of the hospital, the cost of drugs is borne partly by governments and partly by employers and individuals. The mix and conditions of coverage vary by province, income, employer, and even by drug. Over the past few years, as drug spending has become the number two cost item behind hospital spending, the issue has come squarely onto the public policy agenda. Strong unions have bargained drug coverage in their collective agreements, but 600,000 Canadians, largely in Atlantic Canada, have no drug coverage outside of hospitals.

It's likely that drug coverage in Canada will remain a shared burden, with governments continuing to increase support as the population ages. Currently, government programs are focused most clearly on the population that is over the age of 65. This is the fastest growing portion of the population, so the simple passage of time will allow more Canadians to benefit from tax supported programs. The trend in employer coverage, however, is in the other direction. To date, large unionized employers have offered the most robust drug benefit plans. Now, most new jobs are being created in the small business services sector where drug coverage is less common. Large employers in steel and automobile production are in decline and their drug plans will cover a smaller portion of the workforce in future years.

Historically, and to the present day, Canada's major competitor for manufacturing investments has been the United States. Canada competes directly with the U.S. for investments such as automobile manufacturing plants. America has a very different financing model than Canada for its health system. The American government, through Medicare and Medicard, bears the cost for the elderly and the very poor. Employers bear the majority of the health costs for their workforce. The consequence is that the largest single cost to a U.S. automaker is health insurance costs for its employees. The benefit for businesses in Canada is that employers pay a smaller share of health costs. Taxpayers bear the main burden. Companies operate with a lower employee benefit cost structure due to public funding in healthcare. This offsets higher costs in other areas such as transportation and taxation.

Bill Blundell, former CEO of GE Canada, spoke of medicare as the key reason that GE plants in Canada were able to successfully compete for product mandates against American plants. Other business leaders, particularly those running Canadian branches or subsidiaries of American companies, and operating in competition with U.S.-based plants, will readily tell you that Canadian medicare is the single biggest reason they are able to be competitive.

There are other benefits to having healthcare insurance on the broad collective backs of taxpayers. For one, it reduces the amount of "job lock." Employees in the United States are often hesitant to move from one employer to another because they fear losing their health insurance. This creates inefficiencies in the economy and reduces productivity, as workers don't move to the best available job where their talents can be used most effectively. Because the government pays the larger share of the health bill in Canada, the only impact for those employees who shift employers is the potential change to their drug and dental benefits. This is also an encouragement to entrepreneurial behaviour, as those employed by small business are still insured for hospital and physician services. Pharmaceutical drug coverage outside hospitals varies among provinces. This puts employers at risk for employee drug costs. However, they are protected from the majority of health costs.

The future of healthcare in Canada gives merit to considering investments in the supply chain for pharmaceuticals. Individual drug discovery companies are a risky investment. It usually requires 10-15 years to bring a new drug to market. Many fail in the trials process after tens of millions of dollars have been spent on research and development. Drugstore chains carry no such risks. The increasing age of the population, and the very strong correlation between age and number of prescriptions per year, is a winning investment combination. The leading Canadian drugstore chain – Shoppers Drug Mart — is a company worthy of your investment considerations.

Shoppers Drug Mart

One of the best ways of making tortoise investments is to look at long-term trends. As demographer David Foot noted in his bestselling analysis, *Boom, Bust and Echo*, one of the most long-term trends in Canadian society is the aging of the population and increased life expectancy. Put in stark terms, in Toronto in 1920, the average life expectancy was 55, but in the 1950s it was 65. Most Canadians living today will celebrate an 80th birthday. Combine increased life expectancies with the phenomenal growth in the pharmaceutical industry and the drug benefit coverage available, and you have a long-term trend that underpins the successful growth and development of Shoppers Drug Mart.

While the pharmacy is key at Shoppers, the strategy behind store lay-out is clearly to sell you a great deal more. As you move through any Shoppers store towards the prescription desk, which is located at the back, you pass rows and rows of non-prescription product areas: the makeup counter, the magazine rack, the many items for your bathroom, shaving products, and numerous non-prescription medicines. Most Shoppers Drug Marts also stock basic food stuffs so you can pick up the proverbial quart of milk, rather than having to go to the supermarket.

Shoppers has been a successful growth story for many years. It went through a privatization sale to the American firm Kohlberg Krans Roberts (KKR), and then a resale by KKR, at an enormous profit, back to investors. I began buying Shoppers at the $25-26 range. I did not expect rapid growth in the share price, but tortoise-like progress of a dollar or two a year. I was not right, but I was not disappointed. Shoppers' shares have moved steadily higher. Over the two years that we at Lawrence Decter Investment Counsel have been owners on behalf of our clients, Shoppers shares have moved into the $55 range. We see few clouds on the horizon for Shoppers as a business. We believe that much of the value in the business is now fully, or nearly fully, reflected in the share price. This may limit any gains in the near term. The long-term is another story. Our main reasons for thinking that Shoppers will prove an excellent long-term investment are:

1. They have a dominant drugstore chain position in much of Canada. It is important to acknowledge that the Jean Coutu chain is the dominant player in Quebec, but in the rest of Canada, Shoppers has the largest market share, the best locations and the highest brand recognition.

2. The trend to increased spending on pharmaceuticals will continue. In recent years, drug spending in Canada has surpassed spending on physicians. Remarkable as it seems, physicians actually receive less of total health budget spending than pharmaceuticals. The doctors prescribing drugs get less of the budget than the companies making and distributing the drugs. Good news for Shoppers!

3. Shoppers has shown enormous skill as a retailer by adding to the spending per customer in terms of store design and location, and the range of products they carry.

4. In addition to drug sales, there are increasing sales of medical devices. During the SARS scare in Toronto, I witnessed massive sales of very expensive digital thermometers that enabled people to do their own SARS testing without leaving their homes to go the hospital. A continuing stream of innovations relying on new chip-based technologies will allow patients to take more control of their own health. These monitoring devices will be sold — you guessed it — at Shoppers.

5. Shoppers have done a brilliant job of providing an in-

formed patient experience. They don't simply stick labels on pill bottles that note, "Take after meals" or "Take three a day." Through their HealthWATCH service, Shoppers provides significant information to patients. This is exactly what most modern patients are looking for: an informed experience.

Those expecting to double their money overnight will be disappointed if they invest in Shoppers. Those willing to accept long-term steady growth and a doubling of their money in five to ten years will be quite happy. Shoppers Drug Mart is an excellent choice for those content to be the winning tortoise. For the hares, it is not nearly daring enough.

Shoppers Drug Mart Corporation (SC)

Symbol	Exchanges	Market Cap	Price (12 Mo High)	Price (12 Mo Low)	Yield	P/E
SC	T	$11.5 billion	$58.1	$46.6	1.62%	22.6

Shoppers Drug Mart Corporation is a licensor of full-service retail drugstores that operate under the name Shoppers Drug Mart (Pharmaprix in Quebec). At year-end, there were 950 locations throughout Canada owned and operated by the company's licensees. Along with their drugstore network, the company also owns and operates 51 Shoppers HomeHealth-Care stores. These stores sell medical equipment and assisted-living devices to institutional and retail customers. Shoppers, through its retail network, offers a line of front store merchandise such as over-the-counter medications, health and beauty aids, cosmetics and fragrances, everyday household needs and seasonal products. The company also markets a range of private label products under the trademarks, Life Brand and Quo, as well as the HealthWATCH program, which gives patients counselling on medication and disease management. Shoppers also offers customers a loyalty card program under the name Shoppers Optimum.

Reasons to Buy:
- Aging population with increasing drug needs
- Last year in Canada, drug sales were up 11%
- Shoppers has brilliant business strategy to leverage pre-scription drug sales into other items, such as cosmetics, and basic food and home products
- Q1 2008 revenue grew to $2.02 billion from $1.84 billion in Q1 2007
- Q1 2008 profit jumped from $55 million to $101 million in the same period

Risks:
- May be priced to perfection
- Recent Ontario government efforts to curtail drug costs may hurt margins in the short-term

(www.shoppersdrugmart.ca)

Boring is a Virtue

Peace, order and government healthcare may strike some as boring, but when it comes to investing, boring can be a virtue. Canada's ability to cover all of its citizens for most health-care costs provides security. It also allows the sharing of the burden of health costs without creating rigidities in labour markets where employees cannot move from one employer to another for fear of losing their health insurance. Canada's ability to attract skilled immigrants rests on the firm pillars of economic opportunity, and peace, order, and good govern-ment!

6 The Canadian Play on China

Late in 2005, Lord Chris Patten, Chancellor of Oxford University, came to speak to the Oxford Society of Toronto. Lord Patten nearly became prime minister of England after serving as a minister in Margaret Thatcher's Conservative cabinet. Later, he came to the world's attention as the last British governor of Hong Kong. Serving at the expiry of Britian's hundred-year lease on the colony gave Lord Patten a front row seat during the emergence of China and India. His views on Asia stem from a thoughtful historical perspective.

One of Lord Patten's insights was particularly powerful. He noted that for eighteen of the last twenty centuries, the combined economies of China and India equalled more than 50% of the world economy. Only in the 19th and 20th centuries did their world dominance dramatically decline. At their lowest moment, these nations had been reduced to as little as 7% of the world economy. In the latter part of the 20th century, and continuing into the early years of the 21st century, China and India have resurged. They now represent nearly 20% of the world economy. Lord Patten noted that most experts expect this growth to continue at a much faster pace than the growth of the rest of the world economy. As a consequence, by the middle of the 21st century, China and India will be approaching one third of the world economy. Among the provocative questions posed by Lord Patten: were the 19th and 20th centuries the aberration in a longer term pattern of dominance by India and China of the world economy? Will China and India return to representing 50% of the world economy by the year 2100?

Whether India and China completely regain their role as a combined dominant force in the world economy or not, the important reality for an investor is that much of what China and India need to buy to expand their economies lies beneath Canadian soil. Metals — copper to wire networks, zinc to galvanize, nickel for stainless steel, coal, oil and uranium for energy, and potash to increase the productivity of the land — are needed by China and India, and all are available, in abundance, in Canada. As well, some of what China and India need to feed growing populations grows within our soil – grains, pulse crops and other foods. This is a key investment thesis of this book, and the core argument of this chapter: that the growing economies of India and China create solid investment opportunities in Canadian companies.

Why not invest directly in China and India?

Tsingtao — A Sobering Lesson in Investing Directly in China

Investing in China directly can be tricky. My own early experience, which is detailed in *Million Dollar Strategy*, underscores some of the pitfalls. That experience, which took place in Vancouver in 1994, is recounted below.

Tsingtao Brewery Company Limited, a Chinese company that manufactures a highly drinkable beer, provided me with a lesson in the perils of simple assumptions. I have been a longtime fan of both Chinese cuisine and beer, especially since my consulting tour of China in the summer of 1990.

Tsingtao is a golden beer brewed in China and served, in bright green bottles, worldwide in Chinese restaurants. My travels convinced me that an economic revolution was taking place in China. In 1990, throughout the great cities of China, an industrial and information transformation of unbelievable scale was underway. There were 1.2 billion Chinese. Tens of thousands of factories and commercial buildings were under construction to put the new China to work. Industrial workers and the newly wealthy Chinese business class had great thirst. They loved beer. When I considered all of these facts, investing in a Chinese brewing company seemed very attractive. There was, alas, no way of doing so when I returned to Canada.

Three years later, I learned that Tsingtao Brewery was issuing shares to the public. I hounded my broker, the affable Allan Matthews, to make a purchase. It wasn't easy, but after some delay, he was able to purchase 20,000 shares of the company for my RRSP. The cost was $3.60 (Hong Kong dollars) per share – roughly $0.90 CDN – for a total cost of $17,600. I was delighted to have this stake in the explosive economy that was halfway around the world.

With all those thirsty, beer-loving Chinese, I was certain Tsingtao would be a great investment. Its shares rose, further confirming my faith. But five months later, in Vancouver, that faith received a sudden jolt.

Wilson Parasiuk, a longtime friend, is a remarkable Canadian — a Rhodes Scholar, a socialist, and an entrepreneur – an unlikely combination. Among his many accomplishments: the development of an award-winning town in northern Manitoba, a water slide in Quebec, and a hospital in Beijing, China. Willy, as he is known, is extraordinarily well-travelled and well-connected in Asia. In January 1994, Willy was Chair and Chief Executive Officer of the British Columbia Trade Development Corporation, and I was on a business trip in Vancouver. I called him. As it turned out, he was entertaining a trade delegation visiting from Shanghai. I joined them for dinner to chat about my field of expertise at the time, Canadian healthcare.

The dinner was held in a private room at one of the Asian hotels that glitter on Vancouver's waterfront. Eight or nine of us were seated, Chinese style, at a circular table equipped with a turntable. The waiter arrived to take drink orders as I was expounding to the Chinese trade delegate next to me on my enormous respect for China's economic potential. To prove my convictions, I had mentioned my personal investment in Tsingtao. My Chinese colleague nodded and smiled. When the waiter asked for Willy's order, he asked for a Tsingtao. So did I. Then each member of the Chinese delegation ordered a beer: two Molson Canadians, two Heinekens, one Labatt Blue, and a Dortmunder. In that single moment, I realized the flaw in my Chinese beer investment plan. As their incomes increased, Chinese people would switch to premium foreign brands, not drink more of their domestic beer.

After that enlightening Vancouver dinner, I immediately called my broker and demanded he sell all 20,000 shares. He did; the price was $1.599 on January 10, 1994, so my total proceeds, after commissions, were $30,942. My broker was as mystified by my urgent sale as he had been my insistence on the initial purchase, though he did comment favourably on the $13,274 profit (a 75% gain over the original cost). Not a bad six-month adventure in Chinese beer!

An intriguing footnote to my Tsingtao adventure appeared in a May 1997 *Forbes* magazine article on China:

> Consider Tsingtao Brewing Company. Foreign investors fought to get in line when Tsingtao announced that it would sell Class B shares in 1993 – and with reason. Founded in 1903, Tsingtao is one of China's few recognizable brand names. Beer consumption has been climbing in the vast Chinese market. When Tsingtao's Class B offering hit the Hong Kong marker in mid-1993, it was 111 times oversubscribed; the stock shot from 36 cents to a high of $1.10 in early 1994.
>
> A year later Tsingtao dropped two bombshells. First, the company announced that first-half profit was down 50 percent, due to higher raw material prices; second, it revealed that almost half of the $115 million raised in the

IPO had been lent to other, unidentified Chinese companies instead of being invested in plant expansion as the ordering prospectus had promised. Today the stock trades near its $0.36-a-share IPO price. Says Nicholas Ladry, a China economist at a Brookings Institution: "Tsingtao is the most blatant example of all that's wrong with Chinese stocks."

My success was sweeter knowing what a narrow escape I had. The Tsingtao story illustrates both the opportunity and the peril of overseas markets.

Furthermore, it illuminates one of the dilemmas for investors who are investing far from home — you have no real idea whether or not the rules are the same as Canada's. You also have very little daily contact with the companies in which you've invested. Given all this, my view has been that the right way to play the enormous growth that China and India are experiencing, is to invest in Canadian companies that will benefit accordingly. A second strategy is to invest in Chinese companies that are listed on North American stock exchanges, because this provides some amount of financial disclosure.

China: From Exporter to Importer

China's rapid growth is shifting its position from exporter to importer of everything from food to coal. This is the result of steady, extraordinary economic growth in excess of 10% per year as noted in *The Economist* magazine. The consequence is a steady increase in Canadian exports to China.

Coal
China became a net importer of coal in January 2007. 78% of China's electricity comes from coal. China now ranks second in energy use after the United States. China's energy demands will rise about 4% annually, reaching the equivalent of

2.7 billion tons of standard coal by 2010. The winter storms of 2008 curtailed coal production in China, and reduced supply levels to a few days. Although China coal's production rose 15% in the first quarter of 2008, imports are still likely to increase. Currently, China imports coal from Canada, Australia and other parts of the world. China had only 12 days of coal stocks in April 2008 according to the *New Scientist*.

Food

In 2004, China became a net importer of food. China has 20% of the world's population but only 7% of its arable land. The country has been losing farmland to factories, houses and roads, as its economy booms and its cities expand. The amount of land the government wants dedicated to agriculture to feed the population is roughly the size of Canada's Northwest Territories — a minimum of 120 million hectares of arable land. In June of 2008, U.S. Agriculture Secretary Ed Schafer forecast $10.5 billion of U.S. agricultural exports to China for 2008, an increase of nearly 50% from 2007.

Corn

China is becoming a net corn importer as a result of robust domestic demand from the corn deep processing sector. In the first three quarters of 2005-06, the nation's corn exports stood at 2.27 million tons, down 68.3% year-on-year, while imports hit 60,000 tons, up 43 times over the previous year, according to statistics from the Ministry of Commerce. As China's corn consumption continues to rise, so will imports. China's corn exports are expected to drop to 2.5 million tons in the 2007-08 year and imports are expected to rise to 400,000 tons. Chinas corn consumption for industry use reached 34 million tons in the 2006-07 year, up 23.6% from the 2005-06 period. For 2008, the China National Grains and Oils Information Centre has forecast a record corn crop of 154 million tons but China will not export. Exports of corn dropped 97% in the year to date and reached nil in May 2008. China now needs its entire corn crop for domestic consumption.

Zinc

China became a net importer of zinc in April 2007. Price, not supply or demand, appears to be the reason behind China's reversal on zinc. Since the end of 2006, the spread between zinc prices in the West and domestic prices in China has decreased, giving Chinese zinc holders less incentive to export.

Other Export Reductions

China is still exporting in other areas, but at a reduced rate. For example, China's newly adopted molybdenum export quotas may cut exports of this minor metal by as much as 30%. The government of China announced that it would limit exports of molybdenum and indium from June 18, 2007, by introducing a quota system and issuing licenses to exporters, but did not note the volume of products that might be exported under the quota system.

The Canadian Play: Base Metals

The base metals include nickel, copper, zinc and lead. These metals are essential to the basic building blocks of a developing economy. Houses and cars all require these materials for systems like wiring and plumbing. Why are nickel, copper and other metals so important? Why would one want to own a company producing base metals?

Nickel

Nickel is in increasing demand in the world. Until 2006, Canada was home to one of the largest producers of nickel in the world. The International Nickel Company, widely known as INCO, was the second largest producer of nickel on the planet, surpassed only by Novo Nordisk. In 2006, INCO was acquired by the Brazilian mining giant CVRD. Now it exists as Vale INCO, a mere subsidiary.

There is very strong demand from China for nickel, largely for stainless steel production. In 2008, China became the largest stainless steel producer, building over 3 million tons of capacity in that year alone. As such, Chinese nickel consumption expanded by 30%. Further demand has come from the non-stainless steel market — aerospace and particularly, the rapid growth in hybrid electric vehicles, resulting in consumer demand for nickel metal hydrate cells.

Nickel is a necessary metal with rapid demand growth, and INCO estimates that in China, this demand growth could average as much as 17% per annum over the next number of years. In the first half of 2005, China surpassed Japan as the largest nickel consumer in the world. Overall, world nickel demand is growing at about 7% per year. Chinese consumption is growing at over 20% per year. It is estimated that China's stainless steel industry will grow at double digit rates and likely account for about 70% of total world growth over the next five years.

It is not just nickel prices that Chinese demand has driven higher. Prices for both copper and zinc are at record levels, based on demand from China, and growing demand from India.

Copper and Zinc

The big picture view of copper and zinc parallels the nickel story. Copper's main use is wiring and plumbing in homes and offices. Even automobiles require copper wires. Zinc's main use is galvanizing in steel. Both of these base metals are in huge demand in the rapidly industrializing Chinese economy. With vast urban migration and ten million or more Chinese moving from the rural countryside to cities each year, the need for new housing is astonishing. Every year, China needs to build the equivalent of Canada's entire housing stock! Despite a major slowdown in U.S. housing, the price of these base metals has remained extremely strong.

A further factor is the difficulty of bringing new mines into production. Across the world, but more pronounced in the southern hemisphere, the opening of new mines has been delayed, causing supply to remain tight. Delays result from environmental approval processes or technical challenges in developing mines, mills and smelters. Also, some ores being mined in the southern hemisphere are of lower grade or of more complex geology. These ore bodies are more expensive to mine.

HudBay Minerals

HudBay Minerals is an old company with a new lease on life. For many decades, Hudson Bay Mining and Smelting operated its Flin Flon, Manitoba complex as a subsidiary through a number of holding companies of Anglo American of South Africa. Like Rodney Dangerfield, it never got any respect. Being a long way from South Africa, and a relatively modest operation by Anglo American standards, Hudson Bay languished. In late 2004, the company gained a new existence as a stand-alone independent company. Anglo American gave up control and has been gradually exiting ownership. HudBay Minerals, as it is now called, is a major zinc and copper producer with mines and processing facilities in the Flin Flon area. It also owns the zinc oxide production facility in Brampton, Ontario and the Balmat zinc mine in New York State, which is currently in the process of fully reopening.

While HudBay remained a subsidiary of Anglo America, its exploration budget remained very small, some $5 million per year. Another aspect of HudBay that makes sense as a stand-alone company is the decision of management to increase exploration spending to $45 million in 2007, to look for more ore in the vicinity of the Flin Flon complex. This is a region rich in nickel, copper, zinc, lead and other metals, though the main mine at Flin Flon has never had a long reserve life. For many decades, reserve life was always estimated at four to six years.

My late father, a surgeon, visited Flin Flon in my youth. He described it as looking like a shanty town. No one was willing to invest in exterior improvements, though inside, homes often featured expensive televisions and furniture — things that could be moved if the mine came to an end. Four to six years of ore reserves meant miners were always prepared to move on. However, the mining complex and town has continued for 77 years. The exploration investment of $45 million — a huge boost from a historical level of $5-10 million per year — will likely further extend reserve life. As a stand-alone company, reserve life is more important to credibility. It now sits at nine years.

Hudbay Minerals Inc (HBM)

Symbol	Exchanges	Market Cap	Price (12 Mo High)	Price (12 Mo Low)	Yield	P/E
HBM	T	$2.4 billion	$29.63	$9.00		10.67

HudBay Minerals is a vertically integrated base metals mining and smelting company. Its principal properties are in Manitoba. As of January 2005, its mines had aggregate estimated, proven and probable reserves of 21.6 million tons of ore. HudBay Minerals produces zinc and copper products from concentrate sourced from these mines and from concentrates purchased from other parties. HudBay Minerals also owns development projects in the State of New York and in the Province of Nova Scotia, as well as exploration projects in Manitoba and Saskatchewan.

Reasons to Buy:
• Zinc and copper producer based in Flin Flon
• Spin-off from Anglo American now under local management and largely Canadian ownership
• New bodies being discovered in the Flin Flon and Snow Lake Basin areas

Risks:
• Copper and zinc price may weaken

- Costs of environmental upgrading copper smelter may total $750 million
- Purchase of Skye Resources may drain HudBay Treasury

(www.hudbayminerals.com)

Teck Cominco Limited

Much larger than HudBay, Teck Cominco is another strong Canadian company in metals. Investors who had the wisdom to acquire Teck Cominco in early 2003 have enjoyed a huge run as the share prices after splits is now above $90.

Teck Cominco Limited (TCK.B)

Symbol	Exchanges	Market Cap	Price (12 Mo High)	Price (12 Mo Low)	Yield	P/E
TCK.B	T	$18.9 billion	$53.35	$28.00	2.29%	24.0

Teck Cominco is engaged in mining and activities such as exploration, development, processing, smelting and refining. The company's primary products are copper, metallurgical coal, and zinc, but it also produces gold, lead, indium and germanium. The latter three are by-products of Teck Cominco's zinc mining and refining business. Teck Cominco's refinery in Trail, B.C., is a large producer of indium which is a key component of coated glass used in thin-screen televisions and flat panel computer monitors. It also has partnership interest in an oil sand development project.

Reasons to Buy:
- Major base metal producer
- Strong reserves and excellent facilities
- Beneficiary of Asia demand for copper and nickel
- Recent acquisition of Aur Resources adds to scale
- Coal upside through Fording ownership

Risks:
- Copper and zinc price declines if world economy slows
- Tougher environmental regulation

(www.teck.cominco.com)

A Note on Chile

Among the virtues of investing in Canadian mining metals and resource companies is that the benefits flow not just from participating in the Asia trade — Chile has become the most important player in the global copper business, as fully 40% of world copper exports flow from Chile. Chile has a leading position because of its ownership of the largest copper reserves on the planet, and its strength of production. There are no fewer than 29 major copper mines in Chile. Intriguingly, with copper prices at record highs, one of the best ways to participate in the Chilean mining story is by investing in Canadian firms. Canadian companies are playing a major role in several major projects in Chile. A Canadian mining company active in Chile — where 38% of world copper reserves and 35% of production resides — is Barrick Gold Corp, with 44% participation in Zaldivar and La Coipa. Barrick-Placer is also involved in two other gold mines. Aur Resources, recently acquired by Teck Cominco, has 70% of one venture and 76.5% of another. In addition to growing demand in China, the second strong argument for ownership of Canadian metal minors is that they have a dominant position in the development of new mines in Chile. While Chile is the leading focus for exploration and development of minerals, there are also Canadian activities underway in Argentina, Bolivia, Brazil, Peru and Venezuela. Canada's focus beyond Chile is largely in Peru, Argentina and Brazil.

Coal

Coal, though dirty, is still a dominant fuel on our planet. Newer, cleaner technologies for burning coal or for turning coal to gas, will keep coal in business in the foreseeable future. Historical economics — coal is cheap — will take a while to be overcome by environmental economics — emissions are expensive.

Sherritt International Corp (S)

Symbol	Exchanges	Market Cap	Price (12 Mo High)	Price (12 Mo Low)	Yield	P/E
S	T	$3.7 billion	$18.04	$11.68	1%	8.675

Sherritt International Corp is a well-diversified natural resource company. The company directly, or through its subsidiaries, has interests in thermal coal production, a nickel/cobalt metals business, oil and gas exploration, development and production, and electricity generation. The company's coal business comprises the sale of thermal coal, mainly to domestic utilities as fuel to generate electricity. Sherritt explores for, develops, and produces oil and gas, primarily in oil fields situated in Cuba. Additionally, through a subsidiary, Sherritt holds a one-third interest in Energas. Sherritt also has interest in soybean based food processing, tourism and agriculture.

Reasons to Buy:
• Coal in B.C.
• Nickel and oil in Cuba
• Track record of creating value

Risks:
• Cuban instability post-Castro regime

(www.sherritt.com)

China will also import massive amounts of coal, both metallurgical coals for steel and also thermal coal to produce electricity. Nearly a dozen coal mines have opened or re-opened in British Columbia. Sherritt is in partnership with one of the Ontario pension funds in the purchase of coal mines in B.C. for this very reason.

Westshore Terminals Income Fund Trust

Investing in Westshore Terminals is another means of investing in coal. Westshore Terminals is an income trust which owns the key bulk port on the West coast through which the coal will pass en route to China or anywhere else. The giant benefit of Westshore is that it not only gets paid on the volume but is eligible to participate in a slice of the uptake in coal prices. On the move forward, Westshore Terminals will benefit from not only increasing the volume of coal moving through its terminal, but also from the increase in the price of the coal due to their contracts. The most successful Canadian businessman on Canada's West coast is Jimmy Pattison. He is also the major shareholder in Westshore Terminals. His entrepreneurial drive, business achievement and skills are legendary. From humble beginnings in Saskatchewan, he is now one of the wealthiest Canadians. *Forbes* measures his fortune at $3.8 billion. Westshore is the busiest coal export terminal in North America. As coal prices increase, so does Westshore's revenue. Westshore ships coal for Fording Canadian Coal, a leading metallurgical coal producer. The Westshore Fund does not have any long-term debt, capital lease obligations, or other long-term obligations.

Westshore Terminals Income Fund Trust (WTE.UN)

Symbol	Exchanges	Market Cap	Price (12 Mo High)	Price (12 Mo Low)	Yield	P/E
WTE.UN	T	$1.3 billion	$19.31	$11.77	6.5	21.7

Westshore Terminals Income Fund is an open-ended trust that owns all of the common shares and the main amount of subordinated notes of Westshore Terminals Ltd. The fund derives cash inflows from its investment in Westshore by way of interest on the notes and dividends or return of capital on the common shares of Westshore. Westshore is coal storage and loading company which operates a terminal located on the man-made island, Roberts Bank, outside Vancouver, British Columbia.

Reasons to Buy:
- Jimmy Pattison owns the controlling interest and he is one of Canada's most savvy investors
- Largest coal terminal in North America
- Exposure to Chinese energy boom
- Leveraged to coal price

Risks:
- Leveraged to coal price
- Their main supplier, Fording Canadian Coal, is unreliable in providing forecast volumes
- United holders don't share fully in upside revenue

(www.westshore.com)

Special Case: Franco–Nevada Corporation (FNV)

Symbol	Exchanges	Market Cap	Price (12 Mo High)	Price (12 Mo Low)	Yield	P/E
FNV	T	$1.8 Billion	$23.5	$13.6		

Franco-Nevada is a special case but very worthy of investor consideration. The original Franco-Nevada disappeared in a merger. The company was reborn in December 2007 with the largest initial public mining offering since 2001. Franco-Nevada is a unique value creation vehicle. Its focus is on royalty interests in the resource sector. Gold and oil are its two largest investments although it also has interests in natural gas, platinum and base metals. The royalty model is what distinguishes Franco-Nevada from other resource companies. When mining and energy companies explore and develop new revenues, they face several risks. The first is exploration risk: that they will not find the gold, oil or gas. They also face production risk: that the well or mine will prove much more expensive than originally forecast. By purchasing royalties, Franco-Nevada avoids much risk. For example, Barrick Gold Corp has invested over $2 billion in its Goldstrike mining company in Nevada. Franco owns various royalties and benefits both from higher production and higher gold prices. At present, Franco-Nevada's royalty portfolio totals 285 mineral and oil and gas interests. Some of these are revenue producing while others will provide future revenue.

Reasons to Buy:
- Exposure to oil, gas and gold
- Royalty structure
- Well capitalized for growth
- Low overhead cost

Risks:
- Commodity price declines

(www.franco-nevada.com)

Investing in the Canadian Play

The astonishing economic growth of China and the other Asian nations is straining the production capacity in many sectors. Nowhere is the demand as evident as in the base metals. Modernizing China will require copper for plumbing and wiring, lead and zinc for plumbing, and nickel for a range of uses. Prices are likely to remain high even with a U.S. slowdown. The mining companies of Canada will be excellent investments in this environment.

7 Glowing in the Dark – Uranium

Among five countries that rank as major uranium producers, Canada is the world's largest producer of uranium. Uranium is emerging from a twenty-five-year depressed-market situation. One of the lesser known aspects of the uranium market is that for the past several years, the gap between mined uranium and world demand for uranium was met by dismantling the former Soviet Union's nuclear weaponry and reprocessing the fuel. Nearly half of the world supply came from recycled nuclear weapons. Sadly, this "swords to plowshares" bonanza has come to an end. Reactors need fresh uranium supplies, which mean new mines and expansion to existing mines. There will be greater need, and a greater price paid, for uranium dug out of the ground. The price to be paid will depend upon spirited negotiation between the utilities who purchase uranium and the suppliers who mine uranium.

The world is turning more and more to nuclear power, in part because it does not contribute to greenhouse gas emissions. Recent oil price increases also support a return to nuclear as an alternative source of power. Canada's uranium deposits, and our uranium and nuclear expertise, will be in greater demand as this trend develops. At present, there are 435 nuclear reactors in operation worldwide, providing 2658 billion kilowatt hours per year, or 16% of the world's electricity. A further 28 are under construction in twelve countries, including China, India, the United States, Russia, Romania, Japan, and Finland. Despite Chernobyl and environmental concerns about waste disposal, another 158 reactors have been proposed globally. Newer reactor designs will allow 45% more electricity to be generated from expanded reactor capacity. Newer reactors have much longer life cycles. Older reactors have been plagued by very costly re-tubing and other repairs, renovations that have often been more expensive than the original cost of the reactor.

Uranium is facing increasing demand as a source of electrical energy. A range of countries, including China and India, are undertaking construction of nuclear power plants. In many countries, there are few alternatives to nuclear and coal. Even Ontario Power Generation has proposed to restart construction of nuclear power plants in Ontario. Existing nuclear plants are being rehabilitated and returned to service. Electrical power demand continues to grow, and hydroelectric power potential is limited. Natural gas has become an expensive fuel. Coal is under fire from environmentalists rightly concerned with air quality. This takes many utilities and jurisdictions to the possibility and potential of nuclear power.

Between 2004 and 2007, prices for U-238, the main uranium fuel, have soared from $15 a pound to over $130 a pound. In 2008, prices slumped back to $59 a pound. To date, there has been no increase in production although dozens of new mines are in various stages of development and the nuclear industry seems poised for rapid growth. The swift price increase included a measure of speculation as hedge funds bought positions, however, the fundamental supply and demand situation foreshadows higher long-term prices.

Canadian companies such as Cameco Corporation, Denison Mines, Uranium Participation, and a host of junior Canadian companies are participating in the increased and worldwide demand for uranium. Increased nuclear power generation of electricity will require steady production growth in reactor fuel. This, in turn, will require further uranium mine development.

Future Prospects

Over half of world uranium production happens in just three countries: Canada provides 25%, Australia offers 19% and Kazakhstan, 13%. Methods of mining are changing. In 1990, 55% of world production came from underground mines. By 1999, this number fell to 33%. Although the figure rose in 2000 to 50%, by 2006 mining methods were split as follows: underground, 43%; open pit, 26%; in-situ leaching, 22%; by-product, 9%.

During the 1990s, the uranium production industry was consolidated by takeovers, mergers and closures. In 2007, only nine mining companies accounted for 88% of world mine production:

Company	Tonnes U	Percent
Cameco	7770	19
KazAtomProm	4795	18
Rio Tinto	7172	17
Areva	6048	15
ARMZ	3413	8
BHP Billiton	3388	8
Navoi	2320	6
Uranium Ore	784	2
GA/Heathgate	673	2

Source: World Nuclear Association

Ten Good Reasons to Invest in Canada

In 2007, the largest producing uranium mines were found in five countries noted below. Of the top ten mines in the world three, including the largest, are in Canada.

Mine	Country	Main owner	Type	Production (tU)	% of world
McArthur River	Canada	Cameco	Underground	7200 (14M)	17
Ranger	Australia	ERA (Rio Tinto 68%)	open pit	4589	11
Rossing	Namibia	Rio Tinto (69%)	open pit	2583	6
Kraznokamensk	Russia	TVEL	underground	3037	7
Olympic Dam	Australia	BHP Billiton	by-product /u'ground	3388	8
Rabbit Lake	Canada	Cameco	underground	1544	4
Akouta	Niger	Areva/ Onarem	underground	1403	3
Arlit	Niger	Areva/ Onarem	open pit	1750	4
Beverley	Australia	Heathgate	ISL	634	2
McClean Lake	Canada	Cogema	open pit	734	2
top ten total				28,760	

Source: World Nuclear Association www.world-nuclear.org

Canada's Prospects

Cameco Corporation
Cameco owns the richest uranium mines in the world which are located in Saskatchewan. However, the flooding of the key Cameco mine at Cigar Lake has dented its supply prospects. Although the prices run up, it remains a solid long-term bet.

Glowing in the Dark – Uranium

Cameco Corporation (CCO)

Symbol	Exchanges	Market Cap	Price (12 Mo High)	Price (12 Mo Low)	Yield	P/E
CCO/CCJ	T-NY	$12.1 billion	$59.90	$31.39	0.68%	29.87

Cameco Corporation is primarily engaged in exploration for, and development, mining, refining and conversion of, uranium for sale as fuel for generating electricity in nuclear reactors in Canada and internationally. The company has a 31.6% interest in Bruce Power L.P., which operates the Bruce B nuclear reactors in Ontario. Cameco's 52.7% subsidiary, Centerra Gold Inc, operates in four segments: uranium, fuel services, nuclear electricity generation and gold.

Reasons to Buy:
* Major uranium producer
* Operates richest mines in the world
* Outstanding reserves

Risks:
* Resistance to new nuclear plants
* Flooding of key mine, Cigar Lake

(*www.cameco.com*)

Uranium Participation Corporation

Uranium Participation Corporation buys and holds uranium in storage. The company is a partnership between Sprott Securities, now Cormark Securities, and Denison Mines. Sustained higher oil prices make nuclear energy a cost-effective alternative and the cost of the uranium is almost incidental to the cost of building and maintaining a reactor. There is no vast new supply of uranium coming online, and Russia intends to keep much of the supply they have for their own usage. Shares will likely continue to trade at a premium to Net Asset Value (NAV) because uranium is hard to get. Uranium

Participation trades at less of a premium than Denison or Cameco, and has far less risk than exploration plays.

Uranium Participation Corporation (U)

Symbol	Exchanges	Market Cap	Price (12 Mo High)	Price (12 Mo Low)	Yield	P/E
U	T	$607 million	$17.50	$7.92	n.a.	n.a.

Uranium Participation Corporation is an investment holding company created to invest its assets in uranium, either in the form of uranium oxide or uranium hexafluoride. The investment objective of Uranium Participation is appreciation in the value of its holdings. Managed by Denison Mines, Uranium Participation provides an investment alternative for investors looking to hold uranium without the risks associated with investments in companies that explore for, mine and/or process uranium.

Reasons to Buy:
- Straight play on price of uranium
- Licensed to own uranium
- Strong potential for continuing price appreciation for uranium due to power plant demand

Risks:
- Delays in new nuclear plant approvals
- Resistance to new nuclear generation

(www.uraniumparticipation.com)

Denison Mines Corp (DML)

Symbol	Exchanges	Market Cap	Price (12 Mo High)	Price (12 Mo Low)	Yield	P/E
DML	T	$1.5 billion	$13.84	$6.10	0	n.a.

Denison Mines Corp is a premier intermediate uranium producer in North America, with mining assets in the Athabasca Basin region of Saskatchewan and the southwest United States including Colorado, Utah, and Arizona. The company has ownership interests in two of the four uranium mills operating in North America today. Denison has a strong exploration portfolio with large land positions in the United States, Canada and Mongolia, and one of the largest uranium exploration teams among intermediate uranium companies.

This is a diversified, growth-oriented, intermediate uranium producer. With five active uranium mining projects in North America — three in the U.S. and two in Canada — Denison expects estimated production of 5 million pounds of uranium by 2011.

Denison also manages Uranium Participation Corporation, the publicly traded company investing in uranium oxide, concentrates, and uranium hexafluoride, discussed above. Denison is also engaged in mine decommissioning and environmental services through its environmental services division.

Denison holds a 22.5% interest in the state-of-the-art McClean Lake mill, which is currently being expanded to a licensed capacity of 12 million pounds per year to accommodate the processing of ore from Cigar Lake. The processing of Cigar Lake ore is expected to begin in 2011. The White Mesa mill is a 2,000 ton-per-day dual circuit mill and currently, the only conventional uranium mill operating in the U.S. (built by Energy Fuels in 1980s). In July 2007, Denison announced the start of a new ore-buying program. The program, the first of its kind at White Mesa since 1998, will maximize the efficiency of the mill by purchasing uranium/vanadium ore from third-party producers. Denison anticipates purchasing approximately 40,000 tons of uranium ore per year under the new program.

Ten Good Reasons to Invest in Canada

Denison

Market Cap	$1.5B
Revenue	$76.8M
EPS	$0.24
P/E	28.4x
FY2007 EPS Expectation	$0.05
FY2008 EPS Expectation	$0.94
2008E	0.29
2009E	0.61
2007 Production	700,000 lbs
McClean Lake Mill (DML 22.5% interest)	1.8M lbs (DML share is 405k lbs)
White Mesa Mill (DML 100% interest)	137k lbs YTD, expected 300k lbs
2008 Expected Production	
McClean Lake Mill	3.2-4Mlbs (DML share would be 700k-900k)
White Mesa Mill (DML 100% interest)	2.9M lbs

Source: Yahoo Finance/Denison Annual Report

Recently, Denison increased ownership in Omegacorp to 79%. Following its announcement of a new takeover offer to acquire all of the remaining shares of Omegacorp Ltd, Denison announced, in July 2007, that it was removing all the conditions to its offer, thereby allowing Denison to purchase outstanding common shares on an "on market" basis. Ten days later, Denison had acquired approximately 135 million shares, representing 87.48% of the outstanding ordinary shares on issue. Denison's offer was priced at $1.30 AUD per common share, for a total consideration of approximately $134 million AUD ($121 million CDN).

Reasons to Buy:
- Uranium growth prospects
- Expertise in refining

Risks:
- Long appraisal times for new reactors

(www.denisonmines.com)

Uranium Exploration Companies

There are over 150 exploration companies active in Canada and other uranium producing countries. Most of these companies will never actually open a uranium mine. They will be acquired by larger operators or simply run out of money before completion a mine. These companies are a very risky investment.

For the Tortoise Investor

Canada will benefit in several ways from a global shift to greater reliance on nuclear power generation. The primary benefit will be increased uranium sales and revenue to Canadians and Canadian companies. Canada will also benefit from the export of expertise and services related to uranium and its extraction. For example, Denison Mines has a very strong business unit devoted to environmental aspects of uranium mining, including clean-up of old mine sites and tailings.

Canada offers three viable tortoise investments in the

future of nuclear energy – Cameco, Denison, and Uranium Participation. In addition, and discussed later in Chapter 9, TransCanada, a pipeline utility, also provides exposure to nuclear power but in a different fashion. TransCanada has an ownership stake in Bruce Power, a joint venture to rehabilitate and operate the nuclear power plants built by Ontario Hydro at the Bruce site. The restarting of the nuclear industry will not occur rapidly or without controversy. It will, however, occur, and when it does, uranium producers will be popular investments again.

8 Real Estate – The Land is Strong

In the 1972 federal election, Prime Minister Trudeau campaigned with the slogan, "The Land Is Strong." At the time, the slogan did not work very well for him — his majority government was reduced to a minority. The phrase, however, works well as a maxim for investors — particularly over the past decade. "The land is strong" has been a sensible piece of investment advice, as our land and our buildings have been a boon for Canadian investors. Homeowners, particularly in Canada's larger cities, have seen the value of their properties reach new highs. The value of commercial properties has also soared, far outstripping the rate of inflation.

Two dominant factors have underpinned the real estate boom in Canada. The decline in interest rates has made real estate, particularly housing, far more affordable for Canadians. Over the last decade, mortgage rates have plummeted from over 10% to under 6%. The strength of the Canadian economy and high levels of immigration are also responsible. There is huge demand for housing, office and retail spaces. Canadian land and agriculture is also in greater demand from non-Canadians. Former immigrants are arriving from Europe to the more affordable farmland of the Canadian prairies. Despite troubles in the U.S. housing market, Canada's land and housing remains strong.

Recently, I was in Ireland, and my taxi driver from the airport into downtown Dublin mentioned that his brother had become the most successful hog farmer in the country. He went on to explain that his brother had recently purchased an additional 100 acres of land, for hog farming expansion. For this modest piece of land, he paid 4.9 million Euros, the equivalent of some $7 million CAD — a price that would astonish any Canadian farmer. Farmland in Saskatchewan sells for under $600 an acre, not $70,000 an acre! Some of the vast price difference can be accounted for by climate, and much of the rest, by the massive European Community subsidiaries to agriculture. When the taxi driver asked me about farmland prices in Canada, I suggested that they had not reached the lofty levels of Ireland.

Smart Money in Real Estate: The Brookfield Example

No more telling sign of the times in Canadian investments can be found than the decision of Brascan, one of Canada's oldest conglomerates, to divest massive resource holdings in favour of real estate. Brascan has converted itself into Brookfield Asset Management and has sold off long-standing assets in the forestry and mining sectors to concentrate go-forward resources in the real estate sector. Brookfield Asset Management is the parent company of Brookfield Properties, which is a real estate company.

Brookfield Properties now has 66 commercial properties totaling 40 million square feet and ten development sites. Its landmark properties include BCE Place in downtown Toronto and the World Financial Center in New York. The firm has focused on core markets in three Canadian cities — Toronto, Calgary and Ottawa — and three American cities — New York, Boston and Washington. Bert Clark, the Chief Executive Officer of the New York-based arm of Brookfield Properties was quoted in February 2005 in *The Globe and Mail* saying, "Calgary is the market we are most excited about." He noted that then Calgary had a very low vacancy rate — less than 1%. This was well before $110-barrel oil prices. Brookfield Properties is well on its way to becoming a major global player in real estate. It is already a significant player in North America.

Brookfield shareholders have been rewarded with share prices steadily increasing from a low of $10 pre-real estate, to a high over $50. The current $29 range reflects the post split price. In 2007, Brookfield increased its assets under management from $71 billion to $94 billion, which translated into strong cash flow generation ($1.9 billion versus $1.8 billion in 2006 and $0.9 billion in 2005). The story of Brookfield is a story of exiting companies like Nexfor, Norbord and Falconbridge in favour of a focus on real estate. Led by Bruce Flatt, its youngest CEO, Brookfield Asset Management is an excellent example of smart money.

Why is smart money investing in Canadian real estate? There are several good reasons, but most importantly is the strength of the Canadian economy now and over the long-term. Strong economies generate demand not only for housing in the residential market but also for industrial, commercial and office space. A strong Canadian economy, with growth in wages, provides the fuel that pays the rent for apartments, stores and offices. The rapid development of Alberta's oil sands not only fuels investment in the oil sands but also generates requirements back at Calgary's head offices which house many of the personnel needed to support the country's endeavours. The "housing" of these office workers is a terrific real estate opportunity.

Over the last few decades, the Canadian economy has engaged in a gradual yet steady shift, from manufacturing to services employment. Manufacturing employment implies factories: many workers in a relatively compact space. Services employment, on the other hand, sprawls: financial and business services, and the expansion of Canadian law and engineering firms into the global marketplace, means more demand for office space. Office space is a long-term asset that is highly favoured by pension funds. As a consequence, major pension funds are major partners of Brookfield in a number of the developments and acquisitions that Brookfield has undertaken. When Brookfield purchased a 25% stake in Owen-Wyatt Properties, which owned 24 Canadian office towers, the two partners that acquired the remaining 75% — at a price tag of $1.8 billion U.S. — were both major pension funds.

REITs

Brookfield Asset Management is certainly not the only way to invest in Canadian real estate. There are a wide range of publicly-traded vehicles for investors. The most prominent are the REITs (Real Estate Investment Trust). These comprise a sub-group of income trusts but were largely exempted from the taxation measures that, announced in 2006 by the Harper government, ravaged business and energy trusts. In 2010, other trusts will become taxable but REITs will remain exempt at the trust level.

REITs now allow Canadian investors to invest in a wide range of real estate classes. For example, if you believe that the hotel business will be strong because of interest generated in Canada by the Vancouver Olympics, you can choose real estate trusts that specialize in hotels. Legacy Hotels, which owns in the high-end Fairmont Hotels, has been taken private, eliminating a successful investment from public availability. If you think there will be more business for residential lodges that service the driving tourist, you can also invest in a Royal Host Real Estate Investment Trust — this REIT owns Travel Lodges across Canada.

We are convinced that the immigration of 250,000 new people to our country each year will underpin real estate prices. The level of immigration may well expand over the next decade as the Canadian workforce ages and we need younger workers. Our low birth rate will force us to increase immigration. Apartment blocks are of interest as they are usually the first residence for new immigrants. Two residential opportunities present themselves: Boardwalk Equities, with most of its holdings in the booming province of Alberta, and Killam Properties, focused on Atlantic Canada.

There are also a range of investments available in the property field for those who think that the grey and aging population will require more nursing homes, including Sunrise Properties and H&R REIT. A small caution here: Canadians are not only aging, but aging and living longer in good health — so the percentage of Canadians requiring nursing care will likely decline while total numbers increase. Nevertheless, the retirement residence business is likely to be a growing one over the next couple of decades.

REITs can be even more specialized. For example, Allied Properties specialize in remodelled historical brick and beam buildings. Allied has focused on acquiring buildings that were built in an earlier era and renovated. They own gorgeous brick and timber buildings, popular for restaurants and savvy design-conscious offices. Allied is, in many ways, a play on a very small portion of Toronto. If you love King Street West, Allied Properties owns a strip of buildings along Toronto's King Street West, then an Allied Properties REIT may be the REIT for you.

If industrial and commercial properties in Canada's booming West draw your interest, then a Summit REIT may be of interest. They own industrial properties that are largely located in Alberta. Dundee REIT also has a range of commercial properties, most of which are in western Canada.

Whiterock is a small REIT which drew our interest and client investment dollars. This trust has focused on acquiring small to medium-sized office buildings in provincial capitals such as Quebec City, Winnipeg, and Regina, that have long-term leases with government clients. The investment thesis is that provincial governments are long-term stable clients unlikely to shrink in size over the years. They do not run the risk of bankruptcy — witness Enron in the U.S. — nor will

Ten Good Reasons to Invest in Canada

Canadian REITS

NAME	Symbol	Market Cap (Millions)	YLD
Scotts Real Estate Investment Trust	SRQ.UN	31.9	14.41
Innvest Real Estate Investment Trust	INN.UN	740.5	11.14
Royal Host Real Estate Investment Trust	RYL.UN	186.8	9.71
InterRent Real Estate Investment Trust	IIP.UN	53.3	12.39
Chartwell Snrs Hsng Rl Estate Invst Trst	CSH.UN	936.1	7.46
Extendicare Real Estate Invt Tr	EXE.UN	691.1	9.8
Chartwell Snrs Hsng Rl Estate Invst Trst	CSH.UN	936.1	7.46
Extendicare Real Estate Invt Tr	EXE.UN	691.1	9.8
Crombie Real Estate Investment Trust	CRR.UN	236.6	7.78
Primaris Retail Rl Estate Invstmnt Trst	PMZ.UN	1,106.8	6.7
Calloway Real Estate Investment Trust	CWT.UN	1,662.9	7.15
Northern Property Real Estate Investment	NPR.UN	509.5	6.57
H&R Real Estate Investment Trust	HR.UN	2,744.7	7.13
Artis Real Estate Investment Trust	AX.UN	491.2	6.79
Cominar Real Estate Inv Trust	CUF.UN	948.7	6.48
Allied Properties	AP.UN	574.2	6.44
Dundee Real Estate Investment Trust	D.UN	579.7	6.49
RioCan Real Estate Investment OPR	REI.UN	4,571.1	6.18
Canadian Real Estate Invest Trust	REF.UN	1,717.4	4.7
Boardwalk Real Estate Investment Fund	BEI.UN	2,059.4	4.46
Huntingdon Real Estate Investment Trust	HNT.UN	148.9	13.59
Holloway Ldgng Real Estate Invstmt Trst	HLR.UN	159.2	13.17
Retrocom Mid-Market Real Estate Inv Tr	RMM.UN	86.2	13.45
Whiterock Real Estate Investment Trust	WRK.UN	99.5	11.74
Lanesborough Real Estate Investmnt Trust	LRT.UN	83.4	11.79
Morguard Corporation	MRC	449.6	1.74
BTB Real Estate Investment Trust	BTB.UN	42.3	12.3

Source: *Globe and Mail Report of Business*

they be forced to massively trim their workforces, like Nortel in Canada. Instead, provincial governments tend to expand gradually over the years and with expansion, their need for real estate grows. Many provincial governments have moved out of sole ownership of office property, preferring to focus on delivering services to the population. This is an opportunity for investment in stable buildings leased to governments. Whiterock is a specialist in this.

Assessing the Investment for the Tortoise

How to analyze a real estate investment? One of the reasons for the great boom in the value of Canadian real estate has been the decline in interest rates. As interest rates have declined, the purchasing power of the public has increased. When mortgages were at 10-12%, fewer people could afford housing. For real estate investors, lower interest rates means more ability to build or acquire a new building. Lower interest rates also reduce costs of financing for real estate companies. Real estate is the inverse to interest rates. The higher interest rates go, the more downward pressure there is on real estate values. Conversely, when interest rates decline, real estate values go up. Although, in investing quarters, there has been some fear expressed that recent interest rate rises could lead to the decline of values in the real estate sector, one other important factor must be taken into account. If the increase in economic activity is faster than the increase in interest rates, there may still be positive movement in real estate prices even though the price appreciation is muted by slightly higher interest rates. This phenomenon seems to be underway. Whether or not real estate prices have reached a peak for now will depend on the balance between further growth in the Canadian economy and the stabilization of interest rates. There is, therefore, need for some caution before plunging into the real estate sector. If, however, you have a long-time horizon, say ten to twenty years, it might not be a bad time to begin acquiring investments in the real estate sector with a view of adding to them significantly if real estate prices decline.

For many Canadians, their single most valuable asset is their home. Investors often look to equity markets as a way of balancing exposure to real estate. For this reason, investors might wish to avoid investing in real estate, or pick a real estate class or geography not directly connected to housing prices. For example, someone who owns an expensive house in Toronto might want to invest in commercial or industrial real estate in Alberta to balance the total real estate portfolio.

Exercise due diligence. Pick available real estate investments that are both publicly-traded, and paying out a modest percentage of their total cash flow. Avoid any REIT that is paying out more than 100% of its cash flow. It's not likely that many financial institutions will offer long-term lending to a REIT that is only paying out money to unit holders. As an investor, you want to see that the properties earn you a return, not merely cover financing. A February 2006 survey by Clayton Research Associates Limited found strong returns in Canadian real estate. The survey, based on 1,800 properties with capital value of $58 billion, showed that over the last twenty years, 2005 was the best for Canadian real estate. Returns were strongest in western Canada and powerful across all property types, with increases of over 20% total return in Vancouver, Calgary and Edmonton, a somewhat more modest 16% in Toronto and Ottawa, and 15% in Montreal. The overall Canadian average was 18.7%. Among the various classes, retail was the strongest performer, followed by office and then, at some distance, industrial and residential. Some in the industry are sounding a warning. Blake Hutcheson, president of CB Richard Ellis Limited, warned there might be a bit of a pullback: "This is the third year in a row that our overall forecast will be extremely positive. As the cycle gets a little more mature, to succeed we will all have to be just that much more creative." In 2008, we can sound a cautiously optimistic note about Canadian real estate.

A Final Caution

There does come a point in the cycle where real estate developers get carried away. Robert Campeau, the Ottawa real estate magnate of Campeau Corporation fame, built and then destroyed a large real estate empire by overreaching. We've seen the rise and fall and rise of Donald Trump in real estate. Most spectacularly, the Reichmann brothers of Toronto became enormously successful through their company, Olympia and York, which began by buying New York office buildings at the bottom of the cycle. At one point, the Reichman brothers were major players in the global real estate market. They built the massive Canary Wharf project in London, the World Financial Center in New York, and numerous buildings in Toronto. Yet, Olympia and York collapsed at the hands of excessive debt and recession. For these reasons, a long-term investor should focus on companies and investment trusts wherein the development business — that is, the development of new properties — forms the minority of operations. The large, smart pension funds that have invested in real estate through the bad patches are drawn by sustainable cash flows from strong tenants. You should follow their lead and invest in real estate companies with strong cash flow from tenants. Companies that hold raw land might do spectacularly well in a period of rapid development, but land is costly to hold and generates no cash flow. When development slows, land can become an expensive millstone around the necks of companies and investors.

REITs on the Toronto Stock Exchange
At present, there are twenty REITs listed on the Toronto Stock Exchange. Of these twenty, 14 have internal management teams that focus explicitly on the management of the REIT. Several share their management teams with their related or parent companies or another employer. These include Allied Properties and IPC U.S. Income Commercial. The combined value of the twenty REITs on the TSX approaches $10 billion.

The two largest, RioCan and H&R, are each above the $1 billion mark.

Dundee REIT (D-UN)

Symbol	Exchanges	Market Cap	Price (12 Mo High)	Price (12 Mo Low)	Yield	P/E
D-UN	T	$580 million	$47.39	$31.00	6.5%	1.7

Dundee REIT is very well-managed with an ownership connection to the Dundee group of companies established by Ned Goodman, a prominent Toronto businessman. Dundee's portfolio consists of 37 industrial properties and 37 office properties, for a tally of 6.5 million square feet.

Reasons to Buy:
- Large portfolio of 18.4 m square feet of office/industrial real estate assets
- Sold its Central and Eastern assets to General Electric while retaining more valuable Western properties
- Majority of properties in western Canada (43% in Calgary)

Risks:
- A slowdown could put pressure on Dundee through increased vacancy rates
- Rising interest rates could also squeeze earnings

(www.dundeereit.com)

Boardwalk Real Estate REIT (BEI.UN)

Symbol	Exchanges	Market Cap	Price (12 Mo High)	Price (12 Mo Low)	Yield	P/E
BEI.UN	T	$2.0 billion	$50.79	$33.12	4.5%	N/A

Boardwalk REIT owns 280 rental properties in Canada comprising over 35,800 rental apartment units. Boardwalk is Canada's leading owner/operator of rental units. Total net rentable area exceeds 30 million square feet.

Reasons to Buy:
- Boardwalk is a great play on Alberta rental property
- Alberta has a housing shortage and rising rents

Risks:
- A slowdown in Alberta would slow Boardwalk earnings
- An increase in interest rates when the economy recovers could compress Boardwalk's earnings by increasing interest costs

(www.boardwalkreit.com)

Brookfield Properties (BPO)

Symbol	Exchanges	Market Cap	Price (12 Mo High)	Price (12 Mo Low)	Yield	P/E
BPO	T-NY	$ 8.3 billion	$31.42	$17.18	2.67%	3.08

Brookfield Properties is a North American commercial real estate company. Its operations consist of two parts: the ownership, development & management of commercial office properties, and the development of residential land. It holds a total of 66 commercial properties totaling 48 million square feet, and ten development sites totaling over 8 million square feet. Brookfield Properties primary markets are the financial, energy and government centres in cities like New York, Boston, Washington, D.C., Toronto, Calgary and Ottawa.

Reasons to Buy:
- Benefits from strong acquisitions such as O & Y Properties
- Pursuing large development projects in growing downtown Toronto market & strong Calgary market

- Purchased Hudson's Bay building in Toronto and Bankers Hall in Calgary

Risks:
- Interest rate risk
- Housing and office market downturn

(www.brookfieldproperties.com)

Whiterock REIT (WRK.UN)

Symbol	Exchanges	Market Cap	Price (12 Mo High)	Price (12 Mo Low)	Yield	P/E
WRK.UN	T-NY	$101 million	$13.8	$9.01	11.7%	119.5

Whiterock's is an unincorporated open-ended REIT. The company is primarily focused on strategic acquisition, and ownership and management of well-located, long-term leased office, industrial, and retail properties across Canada.

Reasons to Buy:
- Strong tenant base made up of 52 % government agencies, and the rest by banks, insurance companies and national grocers
- Located in markets with minimal competition
- Long-term leases require limited capital expenditure

Risks:
- Interest rate risk
- Downturn in their largest market, Quebec City
- Government downsizing

(www.whiterockreit.ca)

The Land — Strong For Investors

The land is strong. Canadian real estate, with the possible exception of condos in Vancouver, is still a bargain compared to real estate in most of the developed world.

Canadians should consider real estate as a key long-term element of their investment portfolio.

9 The Utility of Canadian Utilities

Utilities, both government- and investor-owned, have played a huge role in developing Canada. Canada has a long legacy of crown corporations, better described as government-owned utilities. Many, such as CN, Air Canada and Manitoba Telecom, have been privatized in recent decades. Canada also has a tradition of well-regulated investor-owned utilities. Among my favorite investments in Canada are utilities involved in pipelines, infrastructure, electricity generation, and communication and telecommunications. More recently, the cable companies — Rogers, Shaw, and others — have become important creators and transporters of essential services. In an economy that is growing, utilities represent a golden opportunity for patient investors.

In the heady days of the tech boom, investors flocked to Nortel as the investment of the future. The share price soared to $120. Even at that highly overvalued price, prominent Canadian banks were recommending purchase. Targets of $180 per share were forecasted by investment analysts. When Nortel plummeted to less than $1 per share, millions of investors lost billions of dollars. In the same time period, TransCanada Pipelines, a "boring" natural gas pipeline company with dividends and solid earnings, could have been purchased for $12 per share — roughly ten shares for the price of one Nortel share. It would have been an excellent trade. Over the next six years, TransCanada shares tripled in value while Nortel shares lost well over 90% of their value. You would still be better off with TransCanada — more than 100 times better off if you switched at the peak of Nortel's over-valuation. Utilities have great long-term assets and strong competitive positions in regulated markets.

In the 1967 movie *The Graduate,* the whisper of future fortune is "plastics." For Canadian investors, the long haul whisper could be "utilities." Anyone who purchased shares in Ontario-based gas utility Enbridge in the 1950s when it first became a public company, would have been rewarded with a return in excess of 13% per annum over the next fifty years. This 13% rate of return exceeds the returns of many higher profile companies. It is vastly higher than the negative returns on temporary high-flyers like Nortel and other market darlings.

Legendary American investor, Warren Buffet has been dubbed the Oracle of Omaha for his fifty-year genius at picking winning companies. In March 2006, Buffet made his largest investment in eight years. He bought a utility! Buffet's Berkshire Hathaway, through its MidAmerican Energy Holdings unit, paid over $5 billion for PacifiCorp, a northwest electric utility. When you're buying utility shares, you're in good company.

Let's consider pipeline company investments. Although a number of pipelines have converted to income trusts, TransCanada Pipelines and Enbridge remain independent companies. Recently Terasen, formerly BC Gas, was the subject of a successful takeover bid by Kinder Morgan of the United States. Kinder Morgan then spun out some of its acquisition to Fortis. Three pipeline trusts, Pembina Pipe, Interpipe and

Fort Chicago, are utilities organized in a trust form. Keyera Facilities is organized as a trust but owns gas gathering systems and processing facilities, rather than main pipelines.

Among the other utilities are telephone companies of which TELUS, representing the merger of Alberta and BC Telecom companies, is probably the most competitive. There is also Manitoba Telecom and Bell Aliant in Atlantic Canada. Bell Canada Enterprises, the goliath which owns the bulk of phone services in Ontario and Quebec, is being swallowed up by the Ontario Teachers' Pension Fund and other private investors. There are also utilities such as Fortis, involved in the generation of electric power in Newfoundland, British Columbia, Alberta and Belize. And TransAlta is involved in electricity development and other utility operations in Alberta.

The basic logic to utility investments is that utilities are extremely hard to replicate. The TransCanada pipeline, through which natural gas flows east in Canada from the Western Canadian Sedimentary Basin to consuming markets in Ontario and Quebec, was built in the 1950s and would cost billions more than its original cost to duplicate. It is well-maintained by TransCanada Pipelines. The natural gas it transports is an essential commodity and continues to increase in value. Without it, we easterners would "freeze in the dark," as Alberta bumper stickers suggested during the National Energy Program. Utilities, with their steady dividends and their conservative management, are an ideal opportunity for long-term investors.

The alternative title for this chapter was "Boring Stocks You Should Love." But the word "boring" is not generally a good idea. Investors, however, should love boring, because boring often links with profitable in the case of utilities.

TransCanada Pipelines
In January 1998, TransCanada Pipelines and Alberta's NOVA Corp announced a merger of equals. This $14-billion deal, one of the largest in the Canadian energy sector's history,

could have created the fourth-largest pipeline company in North America, with approximately 6,000 employees. Trans-Canada kept the pipelines and the related assets, but it set up NOVA's chemical business as a separate public company and spun it out to shareholders as a special dividend. Rising financing costs and the debt assumed for the deal caused TransCanada to sell many of the acquired assets, including the money-losing gas marketing business. In 2000, the cost of the debt forced TransCanada to cut its annual dividend to $0.80 per share from $1.12. TransCanada used the cash from the dividend cut and the sale of assets to slash debt from 2.4 times equity to 1.5 times equity. A mighty stalwart of reliable dividend payments had been humbled. Portfolio managers who had bought TransCanada for the dividend dumped it, triggering a sell-off. The share price plummeted from over $20.00 to a mere $11.00.

Investors fled. So concerned were investors that they dropped the price of TransAlta, another pipeline utility, on the rather weak theory that TransAlta would also cut its dividend. Out of sympathy? Just for fun? Companies only cut long-standing dividends for one reason: they must; their bankers have read them the riot act and cut off their borrowing corporately, and rating agencies stand poised to downgrade their debt rating. Only then does a dividend cut ensue.

At that moment, true value investors ramp up their courage and wade, not into the fray, but into the numbers. Was TransCanada permanently hobbled by debt or would it recover? If so, how quickly?

Here's the story the numbers told. TransCanada could readily chew through the debt by selling assets. At low teen prices — $11.12 — TransCanada seemed a huge bargain. We bought shares of TRP for our clients over several years. Gradually, the share price recovered. Through the years of the tech meltdown, when Nortel dropped from the giddy heights of $120 per share all the way to the $0.99 dustbin, I continued to buy TransCanada. It continued to climb.

Ten Good Reasons to Invest in Canada

New clients, often dragging battered portfolios to our "recovery program" would be treated to my often repeated but mercifully brief speech on TransCanada. "Boring, but it pays 4% per year in dividends at $1.00 per share. I anticipate the share price might go up a further dollar. It is a safe, steady utility. And you might earn 8% for your patience."

In reality, TRP performed far better than I predicted. Here, year by year, is the total return showing both the dividend and the share price appreciation.

TransCanada Corp TSX: TRP

Year	Dividend Per Share	Dividend Rate	Dividend Increase	Share Price Year End	Share Price Gain	Total Return
1999	$ 1.12	9.0%		$12.50		
2000	$ 0.80	4.7%	-28.6%	$17.20	38%	44%
2001	$ 0.90	4.5%	12.5%	$19.87	16%	21%
2002	$ 1.00	4.4%	11.1%	$22.92	15%	20%
2003	$ 1.08	3.9%	8.0%	$27.88	22%	26%
2004	$ 1.16	3.9%	7.4%	$29.80	7%	11%
2005	$ 1.22	3.3%	5.2%	$36.65	23%	27%
2006	$ 1.28	3.2%	4.9%	$40.61	11%	14%
2007	$ 1.38	3.4%	7.8%	$40.54	- 0.1	3%

Source: Complied from TransCanada Corp. Annual Reports 1999-2007

Through the brutal markets of 2001 and 2002 when investors suffered hundreds of billions in losses, TransCanada kept chugging along, generating earnings and growth. There was even a silver lining, when the Enron debacle freed up some terrific pipeline assets south of the border. TransCanada added a major pipeline in California to its network, using its strengthening balance sheet to finance the acquisitions. TransCanada also bought an interest in nuclear power generation in Ontario.

The Utility of Canadian Utilities

Bruce Power may turn out to be either a brilliant investment for TransCanada or a minor disaster. Ontario's nuclear power generation efforts have been a rocky road. Most of the opposition to nuclear power has come from environmentalists and residents concerned about the health and safety of the surrounding population. The real Achilles' heel of the Ontario nuclear industry, however, has not been health and safety, but economics. Nuclear power has been a financial disaster. Plants such as Pickering and Bruce were built and financed on the premise that they would operate for forty years. If they had achieved this result, their economics would have worked well. However, the AECL technology fell apart after twenty years. The nuclear plants have required massive repairs, retubing and rebuilding. This work has cost more than the plants cost to originally build. Rebuilding has fatally damaged their economics. Nuclear power, Ontario style, has become very expensive power. The AECL reactor has been a dubious economic performer.

Nuclear reactors from the French firm, Areva, and from America, Westinghouse, appear to be far more durable. Ontario has recently decided to phase out seven coal-fired electric generating plants by 2012 for air quality reasons, a major deferral from the original and unrealistic 2007 closure date. This creates a potentially lucrative situation for Bruce Power and its 33% owner TransCanada. If, and it is a very large if, Bruce Power can operate its reactors on a sustained basis, then TransCanada will enjoy a terrific return on its investment. On the other hand, history would suggest that the Bruce plants are plagued with shutdowns and repairs — large cost revenues. If this continues, the Bruce investment could be written off as a failure within a few years. The Bruce investment is not large enough to jeopardize TransCanada even if it goes badly. This is a modest investment with a great potential upside, and some downside risk. Only time will reveal its true wisdom.

TransCanada Corp (TRP) *33.16 Nov. 20/09* *52WH 35."* *WL 28.86*

Symbol	Exchanges	Market Cap	Price (12 Mo High)	Price (12 Mo Low)	Yield	P/E
TRP	T-NY	$20 billion	$41.35	$35.13	3.6%	17.6

TransCanada Corp is a North American energy infrastructure company primarily focused on natural gas transmission and power generation. TransCanada's principal operating subsidiary is TransCanada Pipelines Limited. At the end of 2005, the company's gas transmission segment accounted for approximately 68% of revenues and the power segment accounted for the other 32%. TransCanada operates or controls a power generation capacity of about 6,736 megawatts.

Reasons to Buy:
- Ever increasing gas and power prices
- Purchased largest electric generator, the Ravenswood plant, in New York City
- Well-positioned in gas transmission and has a storage market in Alberta
- Building major new oil pipeline to transport oil sands production to U.S. markets

Risks:
- Reduced gas flows possible if drilling doesn't accelerate
- Investment in unsuccessful projects – risk to Bruce nuclear
- Rejection of LNG proposal

(www.transcanada.com)

Enbridge Inc

What could be more boring than an investment in a gas utility? Yet, the stunning fact about Enbridge, the natural gas and pipeline utility is that over its first fifty years as a public company, it has provided a 13.1% compound annual shareholder return. This is vastly better than any stock market index over that same fifty-year period. In practical terms, if you invested

$10,000 in Enbridge fifty years ago and reinvested all the dividends, your investment would now be worth over $4.7 million. How's that for boring?

[handwritten: +44.20 Nov. 20/09   52wH +44.77   L +33.80]

Enbridge Inc (ENB)

Symbol	Exchanges	Market Cap	Price (12 Mo High)	Price (12 Mo Low)	Yield	P/E
ENB	T-NY	$11.6 billion	$38.82	$31.92	3.47%	19.92

Enbridge is an energy delivery company which supplies natural and crude oil used to heat homes, power transportation systems and provide fuel and feedstock for industry. Enbridge's operations are divided up into five business segments: Liquid Pipelines, which owns and operates a portion of the Canadian crude oil pipeline system such as the Athabasca System; Gas Pipelines, which includes the Alliance Pipeline in the U.S.; Vector Pipeline and Enbridge Offshore Pipelines; Sponsored Investments, which includes investments in Enbridge Income Fund and Enbridge Energy Partners. L.P.; Gas Distribution and Services which include Enbridge Gas distribution, Customer Works, Aux Sable wind power generation, and International, Enbridge's two energy-delivery investments outside of North America.

Reasons to Buy:
- Strong liquid pipeline business
- New terminal development in Alberta
- Steady expansions and investments to correctly supply growing customer base.

Risks:
- Foreign exchange exposure
- Energy price exposure
- Continued problems with gas distribution business

(*www.enbridge.com*)

Fortis Inc

I contemplated investing in Fortis for several years. My initial reluctance was the utility's exclusive reliance on a single market, Newfoundland and Labrador. Fortis owned Newfoundland and Labrador Power, as well as some real estate, also in Atlantic Canada. Even with the offshore oil development spurring Newfoundland, I worried Fortis had little room to grow as long as it stuck to its geographical roots.

In the late 1990s, Fortis made a small purchase in the Central American nation of Belize. Although it demonstrated some daring, having my savings and the savings of my clients transported from the chilly rock of Newfoundland to the steamy jungles of Belize was not exactly my hope for diversification. I waited patiently for another indication that the company wanted to grow beyond Canada's most easterly province.

We purchased a few shares, but it was not until 2003, when Fortis first bought power generation assets in B.C. and Alberta, that we became keen. In May 2007, Fortis made a much larger acquisition. To finance their purchase of Terasen, formerly BC Gas, Fortis raised $1.15 billion by selling shares. We bought as much Fortis as there was cash in client accounts. By 2007, Fortis had become the largest investor-owned gas and electric utility.

Fortis' value has chugged steadily higher since these original purchases. Along the way, it has also paid a dividend of $0.52 per share for a total return in a year of 15.49%. Fortis split in October 2005, four-for-one.

Fortis Inc (FTS) ↑26.77 Nov. 21/09   52wH ↑27.46   L 21.52

Symbol	Exchanges	Market Cap	Price (12 Mo High)	Price (12 Mo Low)	Yield	P/E
FTS	T	$4.4 billion	$29.94	$24.50	3.57 %	19.97

Fortis is an international electric utility holding company. It has holdings in several major companies who are, for the most part, regulated electric distribution utilities, such as Newfoundland Power Inc, Maritime Electric Company, FortisOntario Inc, FortisAlberta Inc and FortisBC Inc. Fortis also has holdings outside of Canada with Belize Electricity Limited located in Belize, Central America, and Caribbean Utilities Company Ltd in the Cayman Islands.

Reasons to Buy:
- Well-positioned energy infrastructure company
- Strong operations in growing Alberta and B.C. markets
- Steady long-term growth through cost maintenance and acquisitions
- Large-scale provides greater stability of earnings
- Decent dividend yield

Risks:
- Hurricane risk in Cayman operation
- Political environment in Belize
- Economic risk in Atlantic Canada, especially in Newfoundland

(www.fortis.ca)

Axia NetMedia Corporation

Sometimes, even in utilities, small can be beautiful, but the real beauty of the small Axia NetMedia is its international expertise potential. Axia operates the broadband network for Alberta, and this expertise is in demand in other nations. In France, the government has decided that broadband should be put in place in all 64 districts, some of which are larger than Alberta. To date, Axia, in partnership with a French partner, has won several contracts. There is further opportunity down under in Australia.

Ten Good Reasons to Invest in Canada

Axia NetMedia Corporation (AXX)

Handwritten: +1.46   Nov. 20/09   52WH $2.38   L +1.22

Symbol	Exchanges	Market Cap	Price (12 Mo High)	Price (12 Mo Low)	Yield	P/E
AXX	T	$190.1 million	$7	$2.5	N/A	18.6

Axia NetMedia Corporation's main operation includes the operation and management of the Alberta SuperNet as well as providing maintenance for other communication and broadband networks. The Alberta SuperNet links government offices, schools, healthcare facilities, and libraries through high-capacity fibreoptics and wireless networks to about 400 Alberta communities. The company operations work twofold, with an Interactive Network Services segment which designs, manufactures and maintains the functions of broadband IP networks, and a second Interactive Media Services segment which provides digital products and services for workforce development, education marketing, aerospace and defense, oil and gas, and health media markets.

Reasons to Buy:
- Global expansion potential
- Strength and growth of Alberta economy

Risks:
- Increased competition
- Technology changes

(www.axia.com)

Keyera Facilities Income Fund (KEY.UN)

Handwritten: +22.79   Nov. 20/09   52WH $23.43   L $13.70

Symbol	Exchanges	Market Cap	Price (12 Mo High)	Price (12 Mo Low)	Yield	P/E
KEY.UN	T	$1.1 billion	$21.90	$15.51	8.5%	N/A

Keyera Facilities Income Fund is an unincorporated open-ended trust that owns all the controlling interests of Keyera Energy Limited Partnership. The company is involved in operating a natural gas midstream business in Canada. Through the partnership, operations are spilt into three segments: the natural gas gathering processing segment services producers, the NGL infrastructure segment processes, transports and stores NGL, and the marketing segments market by-products recovered from processing. The company has interest in 16 gas plants in western Canada.

Reasons to Buy:
- Gas infrastructure trust with strong growth
- Chaired by former Alberta premier, Lougheed who remains a visionary leader
- Yield of over 8%

Risks:
- Rising interest rates could reduce unit price

(*www.keyera.com*)

Inter Pipeline Fund (IPL.UN) Nov. 21/07

$10.59   52wH $10.99   wL $5.59

Symbol	Exchanges	Market Cap	Price (12 Mo High)	Price (12 Mo Low)	Yield	P/E
IPL.UN	T	2.1 billion	10.0	8.7	8.8	

Inter Pipeline Fund operates in the field of petroleum transportation, natural gas liquids extraction and storage. The company owns and operates a gang of energy infrastructure assets in western Canada and western Europe. Inter Pipeline operates four conventional oil pipeline systems in Alberta and Saskatchewan, with a combined length of 4,000 kilometres. It is currently building new pipeline to carry oil out of oil sands, which will lead to over $1 billion of new assets for Inter Pipeline.

Reasons to Buy:
- Yield of nearly 9%

- Pipeline trust with ability to continue current of distribution after becoming taxable in 2010
- Growth orientation with major pipeline project underway
- Acquired gas storage in U.K.

Risks:
- Rising interest rates could reduce unit price

(www.interpiplinefund.com)

+16.59   52wH +16.95
L +11.68

Pembina Pipeline Income Fund (PIF.UN) *Nov. 20/09*

Symbol	Exchanges	Market Cap	Price (12 Mo High)	Price (12 Mo Low)	Yield	P/E
PIF.UN	T	2.3 billion	18.00	15.00	8.34	15.84

Pembina Pipeline Income Fund is an open-ended, single purpose trust that owns Pembina Pipeline Corporation. The corporation owns, or has interests, in pipelines and related facilities to deliver crude oil, and condensate natural gas liquids in Alberta and British Columbia. Pembina's three pipeline segments include conventional oil, natural gas liquids pipelines, Alberta oil sands pipelines. Pembina also operates a midstream business consisting of ethylene storage and terminalling, storage, and hub services. Pembina moves an average of half a million barrels per day of light crude oil, condensate and natural gas liquids, to a wide array of customers.

Reasons to Buy:
- Solid pipeline trust with long-term assets
- Yield over 8%

Risks:
- Rising interest rates could reduce unit price

(www.pembina.com)

It is my view that the pipeline trusts may be acquired by pension funds or other institutional investors seeking reliable earnings and yields that are double those available in the bond market. Since acquisitions are done at a premium, usually 15 to 35% above market prices, investors benefit from such takeovers.

Cable Companies

Canada's cable companies represent the future of telecommunication. By bundling together cable TV, internet and phone service, they are outperforming telcos. To compete, telephone companies are changing their business model.

Shaw Communications (SJR.B)

Symbol	Exchanges	Market Cap	Price (12 Mo High)	Price (12 Mo Low)	Yield	P/E
SJR.B	T, NYSE	8.8 billion	28.79	16.18	3.7%	13.5

Shaw's core business is in providing broadband cable television, high-speed internet, digital phone, telecommunications services (through Shaw Business Solutions) and satellite direct-to-home services (through Star Choice Communications Inc), to 3.2 million customers. Over the years, Shaw has greatly expanded its network and leading edge product and service offerings, and is now the leading residential broadband service provider in western Canada, with more than two million cable television customers and more than one million internet customers.

Quick Facts
- 60% of basic cable customers subscribe to internet services
- 50% of customers are now in bundle packages
- Have added over 400k internet subscribers in the last three years

- 60% North American internet penetration (Rogers has 53%, Bell has 30% and Telus has 29%)
- Share price up almost 70% in last two years

Valuation

Market Cap	$11.4B
Revenue	$2.5B
EPS	$1.07
P/E	24.5x
P/Cash Flow	11.8x
Dividend Yield	2.5%
ProfitMargin, Operating Margin	18.63%, 43.8%
FY2007 EPS Mean	$0.77 (14 Brokers Estimates)
FY2008 EPS Mean	$0.96 (15 Brokers Estimates)

Reasons to Buy:
- Strong customer growth in western Canada
- Dominant position
- Frequent dividend increases

Risks:
- Competition from new entrants – lower margins
- Cost of spectrum auction

(www.shaw.ca)

Rogers Communications (RCI.B)

↑32.05   52Wk H ↑37.50   Nov. 2/07   L ↓25.40

Symbol	Exchanges	Market Cap	Price (12 Mo High)	Price (12 Mo Low)	Yield	P/E
RCI.B	T, NYSE	$18.7 billion	$49.81	$32.92	2.81%	18.8

The Utility of Canadian Utilities

Valuation

Market Cap	$31.1B
Revenue	$8.8B
EPS	$1.24
P/E	39.4x
P/Cash Flow	13.3x
Dividend Yield	1.0%
Profit Margin, Operating Margin	7%, 32.7%
FY2007 EPS Mean	$1.31 (16 Brokers Estimates)
FY2008 EPS Mean	$1.96 (17 Brokers Estimates)

Rogers Communications Inc is a diversified Canadian communications and media company engaged in three primary lines of business. Rogers Wireless is Canada's largest wireless voice and data communications services provider and the country's only carrier operating on the world standard GSM technology platform. Rogers Cable and Telecom is Canada's largest cable television provider offering cable television, high-speed internet access, residential telephone services, and video retailing, while its Rogers Business Solutions division is a national provider of voice communications services, data networking, and broadband internet connectivity to small, medium and large businesses. Rogers Media is Canada's premier collection of category-leading media assets with businesses in radio and television broadcasting, televised shopping, publishing and sports entertainment. Soon, it will rollout Apple's iPhone in Canada to complement its line of BlackBerrys.

Quick Facts
- 6.9 million wireless and data subscribers (52% of revenue is from this)
- Canada's only GSM carrier, covering 94% of population
- 2.3 million basic cable subscribers, 1.3 million internet subscribers
- 380 retail stores

- 51 radio stations, and a shopping channel
- Over 70 consumer magazine and trade publications
- Toronto Blue Jays and Rogers Centre event venue

Reasons to Buy:
- Debt reduction
- Focus on profit margins not revenue growth
- Increased dividend

Risks:
- Competition from new entrants – lower margins
- Cost of spectrum auction

(www.rogers.com)

TELUS Corporation

TELUS was formed by the merger of BC Tel and Alberta Tel, the two dominant phone companies in Canada's fastest growing economic region. Of all the telephone companies in Canada – Bell, Aliant, BCE, Manitoba Tel and TELUS – TELUS remains our favourite. The two key reasons are the prosperity in its home region of Alberta and B.C., and the determination of its management team.

$34.72 *52wH $40.47*
L $29.12

TELUS Corporation (T) *Nov. 20/09*

Symbol	Exchanges	Market Cap	Price (12 Mo High)	Price (12 Mo Low)	Yield	P/E
T	T-NY	$18 billion	$66.45	$51.12	2.7%	-

TELUS Corporation is a telecommunication company operating in Canada. TELUS is a national facilities-based wireless provider which offers digital personal communications services, enhanced specialized mobile radio services, wireless internet and data, paging and analogue cellular services to over 4.5 million subscribers. The company also operates a full-service incumbent local exchange carrier in western Canada and Quebec.

Reasons to Buy:
- Residential line erosion
- Wireless industry going strong with no revenue streams
- Growing DSL operations due to industry growth in western Canada

Risks:
- Voice-over Internet Protocol (VOIP) may further effect landline subscriptions but may increase DSL ones in turn

(*www.telus.com*)

Cogeco Cable (CCA) *Nov. 20/09*

+ 31.90   *52w H + 36.50*
L + 26.08

Symbol	Exchanges	Market Cap	Price (12 Mo High)	Price (12 Mo Low)	Yield	P/E
CCA	T	$1.3 billion	$50.25	$32.27	.97%	15.5

COGECO is a diversified telecommunications company servicing the communication needs of consumers and advertisers through broadcasting, in Quebec and cable distribution in Canada and Portugal.

Cogeco Cable Inc, its cable subsidiary, is the second largest cable system operator in Ontario, Quebec and Portugal, in terms of the number of basic cable service customers served. Cogeco Cable provides about 2,384,000 revenue-generating units (basic cable, digital television, high-speed internet and telephone service) customers to over 2.2 million homes. Cogeco Cable is offers audio, analogue, digital television, high speed internet and telephony services.

Ten Good Reasons to Invest in Canada

Valuation

Market Cap	$2.1B
Revenue	$620M
EPS	$1.99
P/E	23.4x
P/Cash Flow	9.4x
Dividend Yield	20.5%
Profit Margin, Operating Margin	10%, 41%
FY2007 EPS Mean	$1.58 (9 Brokers Estimates)
FY2008 EPS Mean	$2.09 (9 Brokers Estimates)

Reasons to Buy:
- Strength of cable operations
- Growth potential

Risks:
- Quebec market may slow with downturn in manufacturing

The Potential of Utilities for Investors

Canadian utilities, whether organized as corporations or as business trusts, offer terrific investment potential. Canada is still a young and growing country. Utilities spanning the vast geography are accorded privileged position in business. They are wonderful long-term investments for potential investors because they will grow as the nation's population and needs grow. Those utilities that are well managed will provide strong long-term returns to investors. Boring utilities are not boring investments!

10 Solid Financials — from Power Corporation to the Chartered Banks

When asked why he robbed banks, the legendary America bank robber, Willie Sutton, replied, "Because that's where the money is." Investors should heed Sutton's advice. There's not only money in the bank, but money to be made investing in banks.

For most of the last century, the Canadian financial sector had four separate, distinct pillars. These pillars were banks, insurance companies, brokerages and mutual funds. Among the chartered banks, the top six banks account for well over 70% of the banking business in the country. Among the largest three insurers, there is the same 70% share. The two other pillars have largely been absorbed. The major brokerage firms have been taken over by the banks: Nesbitt Burns by Bank of Montreal; Dominion Securities and Richardson Greenshield by Royal Bank of Canada and so on. There are a still a few small and even mid-sized independent brokerages, but the vast bulk of Canada's brokerage industry has been internalized by the banks. The mutual fund companies are rapidly giving way to bank and insurance company ownership.

One outstanding financial firm in Canada that stands apart from the banks and insurers is Power Corporation and its subsidiary, Power Financial. As the owner of the largest mutual fund company (Investors Group) and one of Canada's top three insurance companies (Great-West Life), Power Corporation has two of the four pillars. Manulife Financial has been the most aggressive of the Canadian insurers. A few years ago, it acquired the large John Hancock insurance company of Boston to give itself greater continental presence and scale.

Canadian banking is an oligopoly situation that has produced both above average returns and invested capital, and also relative stability for the chartered Canadian banks. Although from time to time, Canadian banks plunge as a herd into bad investments, the stability of their basic business allows them to recover from periodic losses. Asset backed commercial paper (ABCP) is their latest bad investment.

Canadian Banks — The Big Six

At 32%, financial services account for nearly a third in the weight in the Toronto Stock Exchange S&P Index. Each of the six chartered banks — Bank of Nova Scotia, Toronto-Dominion Bank, Canadian Imperial Bank of Commerce, Royal Bank of Canada, Bank of Montreal, and National Bank of Canada — and three large insurers — Manulife Financial, Great-West Life, and Sun Life Financial — are worthy of consideration. Nothing else is in their league in terms of assets. With the exception of Great-West Life, which is controlled by Power Corporation through Power Financial, none have a dominant shareholder.

The major issue hanging over the banking sector has been whether or not the government of Canada will permit mergers, and on what basis. Banks have advocated for consolidation. This consolidation concerns many in the Canadian public who feel it would increase fees and diminish competition. It concerns small and medium-sized business in Canada for the same reason. The banks advance the powerful argument that to prosper worldwide, their scale in Canada is insufficient. Many point at the experience of Holland, where the Dutch mergers garnered much larger, internationally competitive banks.

Canadian banks are undertaking their own international strategies. The Bank of Nova Scotia has focused on the Caribbean and emerging nations, such as Mexico and Indonesia. Royal Bank has recently entered the Caribbean through an acquisition. TD bought Bank North and expanded into the adjacent northern tier of the United States, in particular New Hampshire and Vermont. More recently, TD made a major acquisition of commerce in New Jersey. Bank of Montreal has long owned Harris Bank in Chicago, a valuable asset somewhat hidden within the Bank from an investor standpoint. Recently, CIBC incurred enormous losses for its involvement in Enron and is probably, at this point, the weakest of the Canadian banks, and therefore the most likely takeover candidate. From the point of view of investing in Canada, the relative stability of the chartered banks and major insurers is positive.

Power Corporation

The remarkable Power Corporation, controlled by Paul Desmarais and his associates, is a fine way to participate in financial services. The business career of Desmarais began with a small bus line in Sudbury, Ontario, and has taken him on a journey to the commanding heights of Canadian business. Power Corporation controls two of the countries most important financial services firms, Great-West Life, Canada's largest insurer, and Investors Group, Canada's largest, most dominant mutual fund company. In addition, Power Corporation has major investments in Europe through Pargesa and in media in Canada and China, through CITC Pacific.

On a personal note, I grew up in Winnipeg. Paul Desmarais bought two of the three most valuable companies in my hometown from their sleepy owners. He saw their enormous potential. They did not. After acquiring Investors Group and Great-West Life, Desmarais had the enormous good sense to leave their headquarters in Winnipeg, where he was able to obtain excellent management at reasonable pay.

The annual report of Power Corporation discloses that Demarais and his associates control 66% of the shares. In addition, Desmarais has made his two sons, Paul Jr. and Andre, co-CEOs of the corporation. The Desmarais' control both Power Corporation and its subsidiary, Power Financial Corporation. To illustrate the profound benefits of participating with the Desmarais' as a shareholder, in Power Corporation the year-end share price increased from $24.20 in 2003 to $40.13 in 2007. During that same five-year period, the shareholders' equity increased from $6-10 billion.

Going along for the ride — being a minority investor in Power Corporation and Power Financial Corporation rather than simply investing in the Toronto Stock Exchange average — has been very lucrative. In fact, from 2000 to 2005, investments in Power Financial Corporation gained 10.6% per annum versus 6.5% for the S&P TSX index. Over ten years, the gap would have been much larger, with the return on Power Financial Corporation equalling 22.6% against 8.6% for the Toronto Index. Power Corporation has been an extremely good place for a minority investor.

The Paul Desmarais business story is well worth reading and contemplating. As noted, Desmarais began his business career with a bus line in Sudbury, Ontario, which he brilliantly parlayed into control of Power Corporation, a major holding company. Over the years, he divested the less valuable long-term investments and focused his resources on the promising major companies. Excellent management and a strategic focus on building the strongest of the companies have been key to his success. The two remaining dominant companies, Great-West Life and Investors Group, emerged as the dominant companies in their sectors in Canada. Both organic, or internal, growth and strategic acquisitions have been a great part of this success. In the case of Great-West Life, key acquisitions have included major competitors London Life and more recently, Canada Life. In the case of Investors Group, in addition to strong organic growth, Putnam Investments in the United States was a major recent acquisition.

Replicating the original experience, Power Corporation reached out and acquired controlling interest in the Pargesa group, which had substantial holdings in a large number of companies based in Europe. Over the years, the Desmerais family is continuing to do what they did with Power Corporation itself. That is, they are "weeding the garden." Their strategy, perfected at Power Corporation, is to concentrate the assets in the most valuable of the companies. Trees add to the value of the companies through both internal growth and acquisitions. The discipline of Power's management team is astonishing. So, too, are the rewards for their key managers. Of note is Robert Gratton, who led Power Financial as CEO for two decades, gathering options worth over $200 million. The Desmerais family understand that paying top dollar for top talent is a compelling road to creating value. Additionally, the Desmerais family is very generous towards small investors. They have not engaged in any of the ego-before-value acquisitions that have sunk many other family-owned empires.

Power Corporation of Canada (POW)

Symbol	Exchanges	Market Cap	Price (12 Mo High)	Price (12 Mo Low)	Yield	P/E
POW	T	$14.6 billion	$41.92	$29.35	2.69%	11.42

Power Corporation of Canada is a holding company with principal controlling interest in Power Financial Corporation. Power

Financial holds substantial interest in Great-West Lifeco Inc, and IGM Financial Inc., as well as interest in Pargesa Holding. Together with the Frère group of Belgium, Power Corporation also owns outright the Power Technology Investment Corporation, a large investor in biotechnology and technology companies such as Neurochem Inc., and Adaltis Inc., along with other smaller U.S.-based funds.

Reasons to Buy:
- Exceptional rates of return on equity over a long period of time
- Terrific acquisition skills — London Life, for example
- Long-term investments in Europe and China with growth potential

Risks:
- Newspaper subsidiary, Gesca is facing stagnant advertising growth

(www.powercorporation.com)

Power Financial Corporation (PWF)

Symbol	Exchanges	Market Cap	Price (12 Mo High)	Price (12 Mo Low)	Yield	P/E
PWF	T	$26.6 billion	$42.69	$30.74	3.31%	13.53

Power Financial Corporation is a holding company with controlling interest in the financial services company Great-West Lifeco Inc, and IGM Financial Inc. The company, along with the Frère Group in Belgium, holds interest in Pargesa Holding. Great-West Lifeco Inc offers a range of life and health insurance, and retirement and investment products to individuals, businesses and other private and public organizations. IGM Financial Inc offers a package of financial planning services and investment products to its customers. Pargesa is a holding company which has diversified interests in a limited number of media, specialty minerals, cement and building materials, water, waste services and energy companies based in Europe.

Reasons to Buy:
- Owns Great-West Life and Investors Group, two great companies
- Growth through acquisition: London Life and Putnam

Risks:
- American economic slowdown could negatively affect Putnam acquisition

(www.powerfinancial.com)

Investment Ideas

As a long-term investor, it is hard to go far wrong buying into the chartered Canadian banks, major insurers or Power Corporation and its subsidiaries. A short list follows:

Chartered Bank	Stock Exchange Symbol
Bank of Montreal	BMO
Bank of Nova Scotia	BNS
Canadian Imperial Bank of Commerce	CM
National Bank of Canada	NA
Royal Bank of Canada	RY
Toronto-Dominion Canada Trust	TD

Power Corporations and Related Companies

Power Corp	POW
Power Financial	PWF
Great-West Life	GWO
Investors Group	IGM

Other Insurers
Manulife Financial   MFC
Sun Life Insurance   SLC

These dozen financial companies are all solid investments for the long-term, and will benefit from a prosperous Canadian decade. Among them, our favourites are Toronto-Dominion Canada Trust, Royal Bank, Power Financial and Power Corporation. We believe all twelve will perform well, and these four will outperform the group as a whole over the next five years. In 2007-08, the financials dropped sharply on losses experienced by the banks. They will rebound over time. We also favour a tiny western upstart, Western Financial Group, for long-term growth benefitting from Alberta's prosperity.

TD Canada Trust (TD)

Symbol	Exchanges	Market Cap	Price (12 Mo High)	Price (12 Mo Low)	Yield	P/E
TD	T-NY	$54.7 billion	$77.10	$58.57	3.46%	12.16

The Toronto-Dominion Canada Trust is a financial services provider offering retail and commercial banking, wealth management and wholesale banking products and services in North America. The bank's operations are divided into large groups such as: Canadian Personal and Commercial Banking, U.S. Personal and Commercial Banking, Wholesale Banking and Wealth Management. Canadian Personal and Commercial Banking is made up of the bank's personal and business banking operation, as well as a global insurance business which excludes the United States. The U.S. Personal and Commercial Banking comprise commercial banking, insurance agency, wealth management, mortgage banking and other financial services. The bank's Wholesale Banking and Wealth Management segments provide customers with access to a range of capital markets, and investment banking products and services. This is Canada's third largest bank.

Solid Financials – From Power Corporation to the Chartered Banks

Reasons to Buy:
- Well-positioned for long-term growth
- Waterhouse integration well-executed
- Ameritrade operations producing returns
- Well-managed

Risks:
- Entering New Jersey banking market with latest acquisition is very competitive
- U.S. expansion has more risk than core business

(www.tdcanadatrust.com)

Manulife Financial Corporation (MFC)

Symbol	Exchanges	Market Cap	Price (12 Mo High)	Price (12 Mo Low)	Yield	P/E
MFC	T-NY	$56.8 billion	$75.11	$56.60	1.95%	17.64

Manulife Financial Corporation is a life insurance company as well as holding company of the Manufacturers Life Insurance Company and John Hancock Financial Services Inc. The company provides financial protection and wealth management products and services which include individual life insurance, group life and health insurance, long-term care insurance, pension products, annuities and mutual funds. These services are offered to customers in Canada, the United States and Asia. Manulife Financial also provides investment management services with various products and funds to institutional customers. The company also provides reinsurance services, specializes in life retrocession, and property and casualty reinsurance. All in all, it encompasses seven segments: U.S. Protection, U.S. Wealth Management, Guaranteed and Structured Financial Products, Canadian Division, Asia and Japan Division, Reinsurance Division and Corporate Division.

Reasons to Buy:
- Strong Canadian and U.S. operations
- Growing Asian operations benefitting from Chinese and Japanese growth
- Benefits from John Hancock Life Insurance acquisition

Risks:
- Likely to attempt another major takeover
- Loss of dynamic leader, CEO Dominic D'Allesandro

(www.manulife.com)

Western Financial Group Inc

Finding a financial firm with roots in Alberta soil and an ability to benefit from growth in that booming Canadian province led to a wide search. Our find — Western Financial Group — is a well-led and managed company that is building a base in the smaller centres of prairie Canada.

Western Financial Group Inc (WES)

Symbol	Exchanges	Market Cap	Price (12 Mo High)	Price (12 Mo Low)	Yield	P/E
WES	T	$94 million	$3.49	$1.94	-	20.67

Western Financial Group is a financial services company engaged in the ownership and operation of 54 branch networks located in small cities, towns and villages across western Canada. Through this network, the company distributes a range of financial services, including casualty insurance, banking products, life insurance and investment products to more than 107,000 customer accounts, including individuals and small to medium-sized businesses. Bank West is the company's federally incorporated subsidiary which runs all of the companies banking activities. Its mutual fund subsidiary, Western Mutual Fund Company Ltd provides third-party mutual funds and mutual fund services. In addition, the company has a 29.3% equity interest in Jennings Capital Inc which is a reputable full-service investment dealer.

Reasons to Buy:
- Alberta-based
- In highest growth area of Canada
- Well-managed company

Risks:
- Very small company
- Could be adversely affected by imprudent lending policies or acquisition strategy

(www.westernfinancialgroup.net)

Banking on the Long Term

In recent months, many Canadian banks have reported losses from some of their activities. Investments in a variety of financial sub-sectors, such as asset-backed commercial paper and sub-prime mortgages have caused large writedowns. However, Canadian banks will recover and remain solid investments in any portfolio. I will confess that we have been investing in Power Corporation and Power Financial rather than the banks in recent times.

11 Transportation – Boats, Trains, Planes and Helicopters

Canada has a vast and difficult geography with an equally challenging climate. As a consequence, it is a natural environment for transportation companies. Canada's railways were built to bind together half a continent, and have been celebrated in the books of Pierre Berton and the songs of Gordon Lightfoot. Some political observers even focus on Canada's founding as a nation in 1867 as a means to meet the need to finance the railroads. Only a sovereign nation could guarantee the large borrowings required to build the railroads. Canada's railroads were clearly an underlying economic driver of the creation of the nation. Political donations by the railroads briefly cost Canada's first prime minister, John A. MacDonald, his job, when a telegram, within which he demanded more payments from the railways, surfaced in an election campaign.

The Railways

The insightful Canadian economist Harold Innis used his staple theory to analyze economic growth of Canada. Innis argued lucidly that the key export and its transportation requirement determined the course of economic development. The staple which lead to the canoe routes, as well as to the founding of the Hudson's Bay and North West companies was beaver pelts, which could be transported by canoes. The staple which lead to the settlement of the western prairies was wheat. Of crucial importance, however, was wheat could not be transported to world markets by canoe. It required railroads and farmers. The railroads were built across Canada and immigration policies were forged to lure farmers from Europe. Eventually, through a series of mergers, two railways emerged — Canadian National, or CN and the Canadian Pacific Railway, or CPR. These two rivals went at each other through the 20th century and continue to compete in the 21st century. But there have been profound changes. CN, for many decades a crown corporation owned by the Government of Canada, was privatized in the 1980s. It is now a shareholder-owned corporation. CPR, once part of the Canadian Pacific conglomerate, was spun out as a separate, stand-alone railway corporation in 2001. Shedding the conglomerate aspects of hotels, coal operations, oil and shipping, CPR emerged a decade later as a pure railway company to face the CN. Both railways have ventured beyond Canada, extending their lines and links into the United States. Both are in the process of becoming continental competitors, and both have done well. With the prospect of moving quarter volumes of resources to parts and Asian goods to our cities, the future looks bright.

The story of CPR's emergence from the conglomerate that was Canadian Pacific is worth the digression. The spin-off of shares in the five main companies that comprised Canadian Pacific is a terrific story for investors. The five companies were CP Rail, CP Ships, Fairmont Hotels (formerly CP Railway hotels across Canada), PanCanadian Petroleum (which merged with Alberta Energy to create EnCana) and the Fording Canadian Coal Trust.

When David O'Brien became Chief Executive Officer of CP, the combined company in 1995 had a total market capitalization of about $6.7 billion. The spin-off occurred in 2001. By 2005, to reassemble the entire package, the market capitalization would have been $42 billion, almost seven times the original value. At the time of the spin-off in 2001, each investor who held 100 shares of CP, the conglomerate, received 50 shares in CP Railway Limited, 25 shares of CP Ships Ltd, 25 shares of Fairmont Hotels and Resorts, 68.4 shares of PanCanadian Petroleum, and 16.6 of the Fording Canadian Coal Trust. Over the past four years, PanCanadian has been absorbed into a merger. CP Ships has been purchased by a German firm.

Since its original spin-out, CP Rail has climbed in value from $26 to over $60. Other than their history and the romance of steel wheels on steel rails, what should intrigue investors about Canadian railways? Earlier chapters discussed the resource abundance that will be making its way to Asia, to mostly Chinese and Indian markets. That resource-rich western boom is absolutely dependant on railways. Potash moves by rail, as does coal, nickel, zinc, and copper. As well, wheat and other grains remain a source of enormous transportation requirement. While oil and gas are carried by pipelines, not by railways, it is equally true that the cars and equipment purchased with oil and gas dollars move into western Canada on the railways.

Another factor of enormous benefit to the railways is the increasing cost of energy. Trucks run on highways on rubber tires with a great deal of friction and use lots of gasoline. Trains run on steel tracks with steel wheels and very little friction. The energy required to move a train is staggeringly less than the equivalent energy required to move the same cargo by truck. Increasing prices for oil, gasoline and diesel fuel have only widened this gap. Railways make enormous energy sense. In addition, recent innovations in locomotion from General Electric and others have produced 20-30% savings in the amount of energy consumed by diesel locomotives. Not only does rail have a huge energy advantage in a time of rising energy prices but technological changes give rail an even greater edge.

In 2005, CN registered significant increases in shipments of coal, forest products, metals and minerals, and grains and fertilizers. The only decreases were a small decline in petroleum and chemicals, and a slightly larger decline in automotive transportation. In total, CN registered a 3% increase in volume and a 4% increase in revenue carload carried. As a consequence, 2005 saw CN with net income of over $1.5 billion, an increase of 24%, and a net earnings increase of 28%.

Asia's resource appetite combined with the inland location of the commodities they are seeking increases rail traffic from mines and farms to Canadian ports. There is a strong upside for the Canadian railways in this reality. As well, the transformation of railways has been enormously aided by the emergence of a very lean CN after decades as a lumbering inefficient crown corporation.

Paul Tellier led the transformation of CN, after serving with distinction as a senior public servant of the Government of Canada for many years. He deserves a great deal of credit for taking on many longstanding inefficiencies in CN's operations. A particularly noisy battle was engaged in before a reluctant bargaining agent let go of the anachronistic caboose. Big investments in information technology have allowed a much more efficient routing of trains. The containerization of much transport has allowed products to move from their point of origin across oceans and by rail to their final destination in undisturbed containers. Major investments were required in port facilities to accommodate containers.

Canadian Pacific has been taking some dramatic steps as well. In 1995, it relocated its head office from Montreal, its historic home, to Calgary, where much of its business is. Canada's number two railway is following the tracks of CN to make itself more efficient, measured on its operating ratio, a well-accepted measure of efficiency. CP has made progress to get its operating ratio down to 74.1% by late 2004, lagging the operating ratio of 61.8% posted by CN.

Over the past five years, CN share prices dramatically outperformed Canadian Pacific, rising to over double its level at the beginning of the new millennium. By comparison, Canadian Pacific suffered a share price drop and then struggled to make headway. The dilemma for investors is whether to invest in the more dynamic, highly efficient CN and wonder if it can continue its stellar performance, or to invest in the "we're number two but trying harder" Canadian Pacific and hope that as it becomes more efficient, a more dramatic gain will be found in its stock. Being prudent and liking the overall railway story a great deal, we have invested in both and will continue to monitor their performance. For those who want to participate in the Canadian decade of what may be the Canadian century, invest in the two dominant railways in Canada. CN and CP have joined the ranks of North American continental railways.

On balance, we lean towards CN. In January 2006, investors in CN were rewarded by a two-for-one stock split and a 30% increase in quarterly cash dividend. This underscores that CN's board of directors see themselves as working for the shareholder — always a good sign for an investor. This move to direct some of the record $1.3 billion of free cash flow from 2005 into the pockets of investors as an increased dividend supports the view that this railway is being run as much for the benefit of its shareholders as for the benefit of its employees and management team. The dividend increase also suggests that CN's view is that any major acquisition it might contemplate could be financed, which is a further sense of its approach to acquisitions.

If there's any source of concern, it is with investment in

rail bed and equipment. This is a very murky issue. Since 2005, there have been several spectacular derailments, some of which involved toxic chemicals. It is difficult to know, in a business such as rail, how safe is safe. Under-investing in maintenance over a long period of time will cause significant operating problems. However, over-investing in maintenance can cause diminishing returns. We will continue to monitor CN's performance to ensure that sufficient investment is directed to the rail bed and maintenance of track and equipment. Going forward, we hope to see a diminution in the number and magnitude of derailments. Although investors should understand that derailments are an inevitable part of running a rail line spanning Canada and mid-America from the Atlantic to Pacific Oceans, south to the Gulf of Mexico and serving the ports of Vancouver, Prince Rupert, Montreal, Halifax, New Orleans and Mobile, Alabama. CN operates over 19,000 miles of track. Not every mile of this track will be in perfect condition at all times, but trains need to stay on the rails.

In February 2006, CPR increased its dividend by 25% and announced it would extend through NCIBs its authorization to purchase 5.5 million shares. During the previous twelve-month period, CPR purchased a little over 1.7 million shares for cancellation. By purchasing and cancelling shares, CPR is also benefitting shareholders, reducing the total numbers of shares outstanding and thereby increasing percentage ownership of each of the remaining shares. Canadian Pacific run a slightly shorter network of some 14,000 miles of rail and serve the ports of Montreal and Vancouver as well as feed into the American heartland on the East and West coasts.

CP Rail (CP)

Symbol	Exchanges	Market Cap	Price (12 Mo High)	Price (12 Mo Low)	Yield	P/E
CP	T-NY	$10.9 bllion	$91	$57.3	1.4%	12.1

Canadian Pacific Railway Limited is a fully-integrated railway providing rail and intermodal freight transportation services over a 14,000 mile network stretching across Canada, from Montreal to Vancouver, and the United States, operating in the midwest and northeast regions. The company owns and operates on 9,300 miles with an additional 4,300 miles of track jointly owned, leased or operated under trackage rights. CP Rail also provides service to markets in Europe and the Pacific Rim through direct access from Canadian ports.

Reasons to Buy:
• Immense western corridor growth through expansion project
• Long-term increased demand for grains, fertilizer, coal
• Westshore expansion project points to expected growth in shipping segment

Risks:
• Increased fuel costs
• Bulk commodity shipment decrease
• Exchange rate volatility due to reduction in exports

(www.cpr.ca)

CN Railway (CNR)

Symbol	Exchanges	Market Cap	Price (12 Mo High)	Price (12 Mo Low)	Yield	P/E
CNR/CNI	T-NY	$25.8 billion	$61.00	$42.5	1.71	12.51

Canadian National Railway Company directly, and through its subsidiaries, is engaged in the rail-related transportation business. The company's track network consists of over 19,200 route miles of track spanning Canada and mid-America from the Atlantic to Pacific oceans. CN serves the ports and cities of the west coast, the Great Lakes, the Gulf of Mexico and the St. Lawrence River. The company's revenues are pulled in

from the transportation of seven commodity groups such as petroleum, chemicals, grain & fertilizer, coal, metals & minerals, forest products, intermodal and automotive.

Reasons to Buy:
- Steady growth in demand for oil service
- New investments in U.S. yards
- Increased demand for forest products, metals and mining, agricultural products and automotive segments

Risks:
- Exchange rate risk
- Fuel cost increases

(www.cn.ca)

Canadian Helicopters Corporation

Successful investments require both patience and an understanding of the changing nature of business. Canadian Helicopters operates helicopters under contract. The original business was based in St. John's, Newfoundland, and consisted of contracts to fly geologists to mining exploration camps. Mining exploration, as a business, experiences huge swings of fortune. When metal prices and gold prices are high, much money flows into exploration. But it's boom and bust. When prices are low, very little exploration takes place. In its early years, Canadian Helicopters reflected this reality. It was a boom and bust company.

Today, it is the dominant helicopter transportation company in the offshore North Sea. In the offshore, business is very different. Major oil companies such as BP, Royal Dutch Shell, Exxon, Mobil, and others, have spent billions of dollars building huge offshore platforms that drill into the oil deposits of the North Sea. Oil rigs are staffed by crews who live for weeks at a time in the cold, stormy waters of the North Sea, often 200-300 miles offshore. The business opportunity is the safe transportation of the oil workers to and from the oil platforms. Canadian Helicopters became the dominant player with, in most cases, five-year contracts to run this shuttle service — really, a bus service in the sky. The main concern of the company is safety, rather than cost. There is no safe way to commute by boat to these platforms in any kind of timely way. Three hundred miles of sea by boat would be a rough 1 ½-2-day journey. In a helicopter, the trip can be done in well under two hours. Canadian Helicopters operates an array of helicopters, but their main North Sea transportation vehicles are very large, safe and sturdy.

Recognizing this change in the business in 1999, we began accumulating shares for our clients in the $8 range. Our disciplined approach to this company has been beneficial to our clients. We have been both buyers and sellers of Canadian Helicopters. It is important to take a disciplined approach because with a company like this, there can be great volatility in the share price. When Canadian Helicopters reached our target price, we sold. The share price subsequently dropped sharply. We then repurchased our position and continued buying. The bottom line is that this has been an extremely successful investment for us. From our point of view, Canadian Helicopters remains a very good investment. As the world thirsts for oil, more and more drilling is taking place offshore. Offshore drilling and offshore success means more business for Canadian Helicopters. There are huge barriers to entry and only one other major company, Offshore Logistics, in the game. Offshore Logistics is the dominant player in the Gulf of Mexico, where most platforms are within fifty miles of land. Offshore Logistics flies much smaller helicopters to carry workers to the Gulf of Mexico platforms. Over the years, we have met with management of Canadian Helicopters, and have been impressed with the improvements to corporate governance. The founder and CEO, Craig Dobbin, a lively Newfoundlander, passed away after building a great Canadian company.

There is one incident that underscores the importance of truly understanding the detail of the business. One day, shares of Canadian Helicopters plunged $3. This unnerving plunge represented a drop of over 10%. The reason was a threatened strike by pilots on the North Sea. Upon reading this news, I chuckled to myself, remembering that when we had met with management, we'd discussed labour contracts. All Canadian Helicopters contracts are cost-pass through on labour costs and fuel costs. This means that if Canadian Helicopters settled with their pilots, they would pass through the salary cost increase to the customer. There was, in reality, no chance of a strike. It was not in the interests of the pilots nor in the interest of Canadian Helicopters. We bought additional stock on this news, realizing that the market was reacting to a situation that had an obvious outcome. Sure enough, the labour dispute settled, at one minute to midnight, without strike, and shares in Canadian Helicopters rapidly rebounded, gaining the $3 they had lost. The lesson to be drawn here is that God is in the details. Often, in investing, success lies in mastering the long-term details.

Canadian Helicopters continues to fly for our investors, although there will be a time where we exit this position yet again, simply because the share price is ahead of itself in the marketplace. It will not be because of company fundamentals. These remain strong.

Canadian Helicopters Corporation (FLY.A)

Symbol	Exchanges	Market Cap	Price (12 Mo High)	Price (12 Mo Low)	Yield	P/E
FLY.A	T	$1.3 billion	$31.88	$20.01	1.57%	24.09

CHC Helicopter Corporation is a provider of helicopter services primarily to the oil and gas industry. The company's operations include crew transportation for major energy companies, as well as independent and state-owned oil and gas companies in over 34 countries. Its subsidiary, Heli-One, provides helicopter support services such as leasing, parts supply, repair and overhaul, as well as supplying survival equipment. CHC helicopters provide helicopter transportation for search and rescue operations, emergency medical services, and flight training. These operations are fragmented into five separate parts: European flying, international flying, Schreiner, repair and overhaul, and corporate. By the time this book is published, Canadian Helicopters may be gone. It is the object of a friendly takeover that will likely succeed.

Reasons to Buy:
- Dominant player in an industry essential to offshore oil development
- More oil exploration is offshore

Risks:
- New competitors entering market over time
- Global recession might slow business growth
- Takeover underway

(www.canadianhelicopters.com)

SNC-Lavalin Group Inc

SNC-Lavalin is Canada's largest engineering firm. Engineers, I hear your gasp! What could be more boring? Well, economists and accountants, for two! Counting myself as an economist, I feel I can claim no interesting high-ground over engineers.

We began accumulating SNC-Lavalin shares for investors in the $20 range. Over the past five years, SNC-Lavalin has moved from strength to strength. The merger in the early 90s of two predecessor companies, SNC and Lavalin, created Canada's largest engineering firm from what had been the two largest engineering firms. More importantly, the merger created a company of 7,000 engineers that would become the tenth largest engineering firm in the world.

Transportation – Boats, Trains, Planes and Helicopters

The six billion people that live on planet earth are rapidly upgrading their standard of living. Across the world, there is enormous demand for power plants, oil refineries, aluminum smelters, and mines. Each of these projects requires engineering and SNC-Lavalin have a vast depth of expertise. Their roots are in the hydroelectric developments in northern Quebec but they have, over the decades, accumulated expertise in a broad array of areas.

One additional reason that we liked SNC-Lavalin in the late 1990s was their acquisition of a major portion of the 407 toll highway north of Toronto. In this deal, they purchased from the Government of Ontario a highway with tolls and gained the right to raise those tolls over many, many years. Not only do the toll highways become profitable but SNC-Lavalin has been able to sell off portions of their holdings at much higher prices.

Another successful venture owed by SNC-Lavalin has been Profac, a facilities management company. Profac manages Canada's postal processing plants, among other endeavours.

SNC-Lavalin Group Inc (SNC)

Symbol	Exchanges	Market Cap	Price (12 Mo High)	Price (12 Mo Low)	Yield	P/E
SNC	T	$5 billion	$61.95	$21.39	0.86	37.65

SNC-Lavalin Group Inc is an engineering and construction company. The company is engaged in engineering, procurement, construction and construction management services to lump sum turnkey packages as well as providing operations and maintenance services. SNC is also involved in the manufacturing of ammunition and invests in infrastructure concessions in various industry sectors like airports, energy, mass transit and roads. It operates in nine business segments: Power, Infrastructure and Environment, Chemicals and Petroleum, Mining and Metallurgy, Operations and Maintenance,

Defence, Infrastructure Concession Investments, Highway 407 and All Other.

Reasons to Buy:
- Engineering boom based on infrastructure investment
- Strong position in China and emerging markets
- Tenth largest engineering firm in the world

Risks:
- Project risks are significant in political risky countries
- Some losses experienced due to cost overruns on projects with prices
- Potential shortages of engineers
- Competition from engineering firms in less developed nations

(www.snclavalin.com)

Discovery Air Inc. (DA.A)

Symbol	Exchanges	Market Cap	Price (12 Mo High)	Price (12 Mo Low)	Yield	P/E
DA.A	T	$139M	$1.95	$.88	-	.06

Discovery Air Inc operates through its wholly owned subsidiaries Great Slave Helicopters Ltd (GSHL), Hicks & Lawrence Limited (H&L), Air Tindi Ltd (ATL), and Top Aces Inc. GSHL is a helicopter company that, in partnership with Aboriginal groups, operates a fleet of over seventy helicopters and provides services throughout Northern Canada and several of the Canadian provinces to governments and private sector companies. H&L is an Ontario-based aviation company focused on providing air services to niche markets in the Province of Ontario. ATL operates a fleet of 22 fixed wing aircrafts offering scheduled and chartered passenger and cargo services, as well as air ambulance services, in Northern Canada. Its customers include, among others, major diamond and base metal exploration and mining companies, the Government of Canada and the Northwest Territories. In August 2007, the company acquired Top Aces for $35 million. Top Aces is the exclusive supplier of Combat Support services to the Canadian Department of National Defense (DND).

Reasons to Buy:
- Growth of northern economy
- Expansion of northern mining, oil and gas

Risks:
- Small size
- Fuel cost pressures

(www.discoveryair.com)

Avcorp Industries Inc (AVP)

Symbol	Exchanges	Market Cap	Price (12 Mo High)	Price (12 Mo Low)	Yield	P/E
AVP	T	$30M	$2.69	$.86	-	-.06

Avcorp Industries Inc is a Canadian-based supplier of subcontract design, fabrication and assembly services to aircraft manufacturers. The company designs and builds airframe structures for aircraft companies, including Boeing, Bombardier and Cessna. This fifty-year-old company specializes in providing custom solutions for the design and manufacturing of tail, wing and other airframe structures. The company has a 300,000 square foot facility located on Canada's west coast, at the gateway to Asia, North America and Europe.

Reasons to Buy:
- Growth of aviation
- Strong outsourcer

Risks:
- Small company

(www.avcorp.com)

Bombardier (BBD.A)

Symbol	Exchanges	Market Cap	Price (12 Mo High)	Price (12 Mo Low)	Yield	P/E
BBD.A	T	$2.1B	$7.0	$4.1	-	37.55

Bombardier is a manufacturer of innovative transportation solutions including regional aircraft, business jets, trains and subway/mass transit systems. It also provides systems and services. Bombardier operates two business aerospace designs and manufactures aviation products, and is a provider of related services for the business, regional and specialized aircraft markets. It offers families of regional jet and turboprop commercial aircraft, and a range of business jets. It provides the Flexjet Fractional ownership and hourly flight time entitlement programs, parts logistics, technical services, aircraft maintenance and pilot training. The transportation division operates in the rail equipment and system manufacturing, and is a provider of related services, offering a range of passenger railcars, locomotives, light rail vehicles and automated people movers. It provides bogies, electric propulsion, control equipment and maintenance services, as well as complete rail transportation systems and rail control solutions.

Reasons to Buy:
- Train business will grow
- Mass transit will grow
- Mass transit and train orders increasing due to shift from automobile travel
- Migration to large cities in China and Asia from rural areas creates demands for mass transit

- Regional jets are more fuel efficient and economical than larger wide-bodied jets

Risks:
- High fuel prices could curtail air travel
- High fuel prices could eventually slow rapid growth in business jet sales

(www.bombardier.com)

New Flyer Industries (NFI.UN)

Symbol	Exchanges	Market Cap	Price (12 Mo High)	Price (12 Mo Low)	Yield	P/E
NFI.UN	T	$438 million	$13.12	$9.02	9.5%	n.a.

New Flyer Industries is a business income trust that manufactures buses in plants in Winnipeg, Manitoba, and North Dakota. It is the leading manufacturer of heavy duty buses in Canada and the United States. New Flyer offers diesel buses as well as hybrids and natural gas buses.

New Flyer is enjoying rapid growth in orders. As well, it has an advantageous and stable business environment in Manitoba.

Reasons to Buy:
- High fuel prices are shifting city dwellers to urban transit creating demand for buses
- Large order backlog of over 3000 buses worth over $3 billion
- Natural gas engine option is attractive to cities seeking "greener" solutions — offered by New Flyer Industries to customers

Risks:
- Labour source availability for expansion

- Stresses on municipal governments reducing ability to purchase buses

(www.newflyer.com)

The Challenge of Geography

The challenges of Canada's geography have produced innovation and enterprise in transportation. Investors are well advised to consider allocating some of their investment to the transportation sector. Canadian transportation companies will benefit from the movement to trains, mass transit and newer, more fuel-efficient planes. Investors can benefit from these trends by investing in transportation companies.

12 Feeding the World – Agriculture and Potash

There are six billion seven hundred million people trying to survive on the planet. Nearly one billion are hungry each night. Feeding the world will become even tougher as the population grows to a forecasted nine billion plus by the year 2050. Life expectancy is also rising. In fact, in 1993, the World Bank estimated that life expectancy rose more in the last forty years than in the previous 2000 years! There is also a loss of arable or farmable land as cities sprawl out into the country. In China, over 100 million people have moved from the country to the city. Half of Canada, and half of the world's people, now live in cities. As such, the land remaining in agriculture will need to be increasingly productive. That means a larger agriculture industry, better seeds and techniques, and more fertilizer use.

Diets are also changing. For example, as incomes increase, the Chinese population is eating more meat. This diet shift results in far greater overall agricultural demand. Meat production requires that grain be fed first to animals. This process of producing meat for food uses much more grain. In the first half of 2008 food riots had occurred in 33 nations over rapidly increasing food rice prices – bread, rice and grains.

PotashCorp, formerly the Potash Corporation of Saskatchewan, estimates that potash consumption at 4.4 million metric tons (MMT) in India is less than half the 10.5 MMT scientifically recommended. In China, Brazil and India combined, potash consumption of 23 MMT (2007) is less than half the 48 MMT scientifically recommended. Their strong conclusion – the world needs more fertilizers to feed itself!

Potash

Potash is a nutrient that is essential for plant growth. Roughly 95% of world potash production goes into fertilizer; the other 5% is used in everything from soap to television tubes. Potash gets its name from American settlers who produced potassium carbonate by evaporating water filtered through wood ashes. The ash-like crystalline residue remaining was called "pot-ash" and was used in to make soap. This process of making potash is registered as United States patent 1! It was the earliest "new" technology.

It is well worth considering the literal ocean of potash underneath Saskatchewan — deposits laid down as the bed of an ancient sea. The main use of this potash is for fertilizer. As the world's population continues to grow and the expansion of cities chews up agricultural land around the globe, there is a need for greater productivity within remaining farmland. The addition of fertilizer in significant quantities is part of the answer to feeding the world's future population. Most base metal mining ventures require the ore deposit to be large enough to support a 7-10 year mine lifespan. Those investing in potash need have no such concern about reserves. The major potash mines count their reserves in 100-year quantities. The key barrier to entry is the extreme cost of drilling a large mineshaft through water bearing strata. The cost has escalated from $500 million in the 1980s to over $2 billion today.

Saskatchewan potash deposits were discovered in the 1940s through exploration drilling for petroleum. Potash is in the prairie land formation, 1,000 metres beneath much of southern Saskatchewan. The reserves are massive. It is estimated that Saskatchewan could supply current world demands for several hundred years. The first mine opened in 1962, when IMC Global (now Mosaic) opened its K1 mine in Esterhazy. By 1971, ten mines were in operation.

Currently, Saskatchewan produces about $2 billion worth of potash per year. Prices have nearly tripled in 2007-08. This will boost dramatically the value of potash production. About 5% of Saskatchewan's production is consumed in Canada, while 65% is used in the U.S.; the balance goes to China, Japan, Malaysia, Korea and Indonesia. Future prospects for potash are a key element in the Saskatchewan economy; they are also a valuable long-term contribution to Canadian economic prosperity and exports.

In the 1970s, I had occasion to visit Saskatchewan and tour a potash mine just outside of Saskatoon. Unlike hard rock, potash is soft and mined by huge machines. A potash mine is an entire underground world, complete with vehicles. Massive rooms are carved out of the potash, which is thick enough to be chewed through by enormous machines which send the excavated potash along conveyer belts to the surface. Another surprising aspect, given the -40 degree cold that afflicts Saskatchewan in winter, is that because of their depth −1,000 metres closer to the warm core of our planet — potash mines boast a very pleasant, vaguely tropical temperature. Because the potash is sandwiched between layers of rock salt formations, there is a salt scent to the air, not unlike the seashore. The life of a potash mine is vastly superior to the life of a coal mine.

PotashCorp

Potash and the PotashCorp represent another opportunity for a play on China's rapid growth. Just over twenty years ago, I visited China for the first time. The trip had to do with potash. In those days, the vast majority of Canada's potash came from Saskatchewan. Manitoba, where I worked for the government, had potash deposits along the Saskatchewan border, but no mine. The price tag on developing a mine was $500 million. Manitoba was ill-equipped to bankroll the small company that controlled the potash deposits. The hope of Manitoba's then-Minister of Mines and Energy, Willy Parasiuk was to convince China and India, whose future need for potash fertilizer was estimated to be enormous, to participate directly, with equity investment, or by way of a long-term contract. This became one of the rationales for a 1984 trip by then-Premier Howard Pawley to China and India. As Cabinet Secretary, I helped organize the trip and accompanied the Premier and his key ministers.

In Beijing, we met with and pitched the Minister of Agriculture for China. He was in complete agreement regarding the need for increased potash fertilizer to be used by the 330 million Chinese peasant farmers of the era. We couldn't believe our ears. I felt a sense of delight that this would be an economic bonanza for Manitoba. It wasn't until the Minister went on speaking, however, that we realized far more than shiploads of potash fertilizer were needed. The Minister explained that in addition to the potash fertilizer our help was needed to build ports to unload the ships. Also necessary were port facilities, a railway to transport the potash to farming communities, bagging plants, and trucks to move the potash fertilizer. Furthermore, he concluded, twenty years of agricultural extension work would be required to convince those 330 million peasant farmers that they actually needed to use potash fertilizer on their land. Our hopes for an early start on a Manitoba potash mine were dashed.

Feeding the World – Agriculture and Potash

The stunning thing, however, is that's exactly what happened. The Government of Saskatchewan, PotashCorp, and the Canadian International Development Agency (CIDA), invested in twenty years of agricultural extension. The infrastructure — ports and railways — has been built. And China's use of potash is now rapidly ramping up. The good news for Saskatchewan is that it still has over 400 years supply of potash in the bed of ancient sea laid down under the province which is relatively easy to mine and transport. So, if Chinese agriculture has a bright future, the right investment is not to buy a small farm in China, but equity in the PotashCorp.

$122.79   52 WH $135 ~
PotashCorp (POT) *Nov. 21/09   L $61.81*

Symbol	Exchanges	Market Cap	Price (12 Mo High)	Price (12 Mo Low)	Yield	P/E
POT	T-NY	$60 billion	$218.50	$65.46	0.2%	

PotashCorp is an integrated fertilizer and related industrial and feed products company. The company's potash operations represent around 17% of global production. Its phosphate operation represents an estimated 6% of world phosphoric acid production. PotashCorp's nitrogen operations represented an estimated 2% of world ammonia production. The company produces the potash from six mines in Saskatchewan and one in New Brunswick.

Reasons to Buy:
- 400 years of potash reserves under Saskatchewan
- Rapidly growing markets in China/India for potash fertilizer
- One of the dominant world players in potash with an ability to increase production

Risks:
• Fluctuation in Chinese demand
• Price declines if additional mines are developed

(www.potashcorp.com)

PotashCorp is the world's largest fertilizer company by capacity, producing the three primary plant nutrients: potash, nitrogen and phosphate. It has the majority of the world's excess potash capacity. Tight supply and demand fundamentals for potash, combined with minimal supply increases, positions potash for further strength in 2008 and beyond. While potash prices have been trending upward for 17 years, the sharpest increase occurred in the last five years, when prices increased from $80 USD per ton in 2003, to $165 USD per ton in 2007. In 2007-08, prices have tripled to more than US $570 per ton.

New mines are hampered by unfavourable economics. Even with a viable long-term potash deposit, as noted, a company would need to invest $2 billion for an underground mine and then wait a few years before positive cash flow generation. In terms of revenue split in 2007 earnings, PotashCorp is expected to generate 35% from potash, 30% from phosphorus and 35% from nitrogen. CIBC World Markets predicts that on the back of strong potash prices, this is expected to shift 2008 earnings to 42% from potash, with the remaining 58% split equally between phosphorous and nitrogen. PotashCorp has 22% of the world's potash capacity and 75% of the world's unused capacity, which the company is bringing online through de-bottlenecking and expansion projects. It is well-positioned to capitalize on the long-term growth in global demand. PotashCorp currently has ten million tons of potash sales forecasted for 2008 but through de-bottlenecking, expects to get to 15.7 MMT by 2015 for a fraction of the cost of greenfield developments. PotashCorp is the world's 4th largest nitrogen producer, with two-thirds of its ammonia production in Trinidad where it benefits from long-term lower-cost gas contracts. PotashCorp is the world's 3rd largest phosphate producer. Advantages include its long-term, low cost reserves and high-quality low impurity rock, as well as a diversified product line.

We like PotashCorp's strong operational discipline, which has resulted in very robust (and growing) gross margins. Overall gross margins are expected to increase from $561 million in 2006 to $2.2 billion in 2008, driven mainly by higher potash prices. We also like PotashCorp's focus on ensuring that its cash flow return on investments exceeds its cost of capital. Given expectations of continued growing demand for food — as indicated by food price inflation — and the need for better yields through fertilizer and nutrient use, we believe PotashCorp is an industry leader that will continue to benefit from higher potash, phosphorous and nitrogen prices and grow its earnings. Potash forecasts net earnings to double from $1.1 billion USD in 2007 to $2-2.3 billion USD in 2008.

Like the tar sands, the potash resource and economic prospect underscores the depth of Canada's resource endowment. Not every natural resource in Canada is in a supply position of hundreds of years, but potash is. And the energy resources of Canada, between hydroelectric generation and future potential as well as the combination of oil, natural gas, and coal, have to be considered against Canada's relatively small population. Occupying a land mass roughly the size of the United States, Canada has one tenth of the United States' population. As a consequence, even though the Canadian climate makes Canadians very high consumers of energy on a per capita basis, Canada's resource abundance is significantly available for export to those nations in the world whose populations outstretch their natural resource endowment.

This is one of the fundamentally strong arguments for Canada over the long haul. It suggests that terms of trade may return, as they did in parts of the 20th century, to favour those with natural resources. Canada will need to develop its natural resources in a sensible way and build links with the rest of the world. In this regard, the potash story is an educational one with lessons for other industries. Canadian potash producers required the patience and the willingness to invest in order to develop the Chinese market. The Chinese market is developing as the Chinese industrial boom is transferring hundreds of millions of Chinese from the country to the cities, in the largest migration in human history. The remaining farmers will be responsible for feeding over 1.2 billion Chinese. The farmers no longer number 330 million. Over 100 million rural residents have moved to Chinese cities in the past decade. Another 100 million are expected to move by 2020. Chinese farmers will eventually be a fraction of their former numbers. Canada, with its several hundred years of potash, has built the basis for a long-term partnership with the Chinese market and to a somewhat lesser extent, with the Indian market.

Agriculture

Beyond the fertilizer business, there are other opportunities in the agriculture sector for investors. There are several other agricultural companies worthy of your consideration. These range from chemicals to grain handling to machinery manufacturing.

Agrium Inc (AGU)

Symbol	Exchanges	Market Cap	Price (12 Mo High)	Price (12 Mo Low)	Yield	P/E
AGU	T, NYSE	$9.7 billion	$116.15	$50.08	0.18%	6.1

Agrium Inc is a profitable fertilizers and agricultural chemicals company that produces, markets and distributes nitrogen-based phosphate, potash and sulphur-based fertilizers in North America, Argentina and Chile. With an extensive storage and wholesale distribution network, it is one of the largest independent retailers of fertilizers, seeds and chemicals;

406 retail farm centres also provide agronomic services. The company owns and operates thirty full-service farm centres in Argentina and Chile.

Reasons to Buy:
- High fertilizer demand and prices
- Recent European acquisition extends retail distribution

Risks:
- Decline in fertilizer demand
- New supply eroding prices

(www.agrium.com)

Migao Corporation (MGO)

Symbol	Exchanges	Market Cap	Price (12 Mo High)	Price (12 Mo Low)	Yield	P/E
MGO	T	$227 million	$11.97	$4.20	0%	11.2

Migao Corporation is a profitable specialty chemicals company that manufactures specialty potash-based fertilizers at three facilities in China for the Chinese market. Primary products include potassium nitrate and potassium sulphate suited for growing fruits and vegetables, tobacco and cotton.

Reasons to Buy:
- Chinese fertilizer demand
- Increasing plant capacity
- Strong pricing

Risks:
- Production ramp-up

(www.migaocorp.com)

Ten Good Reasons to Invest in Canada

Ag Growth Income Fund (AFN.UN)

Symbol	Exchanges	Market Cap	Price (12 Mo High)	Price (12 Mo Low)	Yield	P/E
AFN.UN	T	$280 million	$38.30	$19.31	9.32%	NA

Ag Growth Income Fund is a profitable construction, farm machinery, and heavy trucks company manufacturing portable grain handling equipment, including augers, belt conveyors and other grain handling accessories through 1,400 dealers and distributors in Canada and the United States.

Reasons to Buy:
- Solid acquisition strategy for growth
- Strong growth in farm income coupled with increase in farm storage of grain
- Corn crop leading to more rapid wearing out of augers

Risks:
- Production delays

(www.aggrowth.com)

Alliance Grain Traders Income Fund (AGT.UN)

Symbol	Exchanges	Market Cap	Price (12 Mo High)	Price (12 Mo Low)	Yield	P/E
AGT.UN	T (Venture)	$78.3 million	$16.25	$7.80	4.05%	NA

Alliance Grain Traders Income Fund is a profitable diversified commercial service holding securities in Agtech Processors Inc. Agtech acquires, processes and exports green lentils, primarily to South America, North Africa and the Middle East, and operates food processing plants in Saskatchewan and North Dakota.

Feeding the World – Agriculture and Potash

Reasons to Buy:
- Sensible acquisition strategy for growth
- Strong management
- High prices for pulse crops

Risks:
- Small size
- Commodity prices

(www.alliancegraintraders.com)

Viterra (VT)

Symbol	Exchanges	Market Cap	Price (12 Mo High)	Price (12 Mo Low)	Yield	P/E
VT	T	$2.4 billion	$15.19	$9.25	0%	NA

Viterra was formed through the merger of the Saskatchewan Wheat Pool and Agricore United.

It is a profitable diversified agri-business conglomerate providing sales channels for crops and services sourced from more than 100 facilities across the Prairies. It is also in grain handling and marketing, livestock feed, agri-food processing and financial services for the farming sector. Combined revenues are estimated at more than $4 billion. Viterra provides diversified exposure to the Canadian agri-business value chain, with customers in Latin America, Asia and Europe.

Reasons to Buy:
- Record grain prices
- High import prices
- Viterra benefits from both import and grain prices

Risks:
- Low margins on some parts of the business

(www.viterra.com)

Farmageddon

Feeding the world will be a theme of this century. The term "Farmageddon" has been coined to describe the chaos that will befall nations where shortages of food are experienced. In early 2008, over thirty countries had food riots where shortages of rice, bread or other staple foods caused civil unrest and violence. A very determined effort by farmers, governments and agricultural supplies will be necessary to feed the world. Only 2.2% of Canada's economy is in agriculture but we rank as the 6th largest producer of wheat and the 8th largest producer of cereal grains. Our production and export of grains and fertilizer will be an important contribution to global success in meeting food demand. Investing in Canadian companies in agriculture is a sensible idea for the short, medium and long-term.

MAKING YOUR INVESTMENT

13 The DIY Approach – Building and Managing Your Own Portfolio

I've spent a decade successfully managing my own investment portfolios, and another decade successfully managing other people's investments. But, the do-it-yourself approach is not for everyone. You need to decide whether this strategy can work for you. Ask yourself three questions:

1. Are you willing to devote a significant amount of time to educating yourself about financial markets and the economy, and to monitoring your portfolio?
2. Are you confident in your ability to resist the personal tides of fear and greed?
3. Are you interested and ready to master a new set of skills and knowledge by reading company reports and financial magazines and/or attending seminars?

If your answer to each of these three questions is "yes," then you're ready for a self-directed RRSP or investment portfolio. If some of your answers are negative, you might be better off investing in a well-managed Canadian mutual fund, or engaging a capable broker or investment counsel.

For many investors, a lump sum provides the start to an investment adventure – perhaps a small inheritance or a "package" from a downsizing employer. For others, determined savings is necessary to accumulate a small nest egg. The key is to start investing, so that you can start learning. We learn through practice. Stop buying lottery tickets — long journeys begin with small steps.

Thirty Minutes a Day

How to find the time to study companies and decide on investments? From Roy Harrod's excellent biography on noted British economist John Maynard Keynes, I learned Keynes devoted the first half-hour of each morning to his investments. I followed this pattern for the first 12 years of my investment career, until I turned "pro." Monday through Saturday, I rose early — generally at 6:00am — and fetched my *Globe and Mail* from the front porch. Over coffee, I reviewed the business news, the price of each stock, and occasionally, the bond that I owned. Upon finishing *The Globe and Mail*, I also reviewed annual and quarterly reports from companies in which I had invested. This was a calm time to review my current and potential future investments. By the end of each half-hour, I decided whether to buy, sell, or let the portfolio ride another day in the market. These thirty minutes a day, devoted to the quest for investment success and a more comfortable retirement, represent valuable learning time.

It was with this simple routine that I met my original goal of a million-dollar RRSP over ten years (1986 to 1996). This decade is well described in *Million Dollar Strategy*. En route to my target, there were many mistakes, along with a number of wonderful moments. There are few endeavours more satisfying than finding a company that is doing everything right, investing in its shares, and then having other investors verify your confidence by bidding up their price. Finding value in the stock market is an enterprise that requires the inquisitive spirit of Sherlock Holmes, the determination of Winston Churchill, and the patience of Job.

Markets are driven by two powerful human emotions:

fear and greed. To succeed as an investor requires a healthy dose of emotion and a contrary personality. When the mob of investors is fearful, it's time for some bold greed. When the mob is filled with greed, it's time to be fearful. What must remain consistent is your ability to be both patient and decisive. If I sound a little like the golf instructor who, after twenty different posture-shaping commands, suggests that you relax, that's because investing requires the same curious mixture of attention and calm as golf. A good alternate title for this section might be "Zen and the Art of Investing."

For me, investing is an adventure — sleuthing for value in the world of companies and their equities. I've always been a reader, and the financial world provides an unending stream of reports, studies, and analyses through which to sleuth. I am an avid reader of business magazines such as *Forbes*, *Fortune*, *Canadian Business*, *Fast Company*, *Worth*, *Success*, *The Economist*, and *Inc*. I tear out articles with references to companies that pique my interest. I maintained an "Ideas File," which always provides a good source of leads on which to draw for further research. Many of these leads turn out to be dead ends, but once in a while, I uncover a true gem. Sometimes, I explore a company by purchasing a few initial shares to gain access to their information flow, but this step is not essential. Companies will send you their annual and quarterly reports if you simply ask. Additionally, the internet is teeming with information on thousands of companies; corporate websites often contain up-to-the minute press releases, as well as timely quarterly and special reports. To ensure trends are positive, the wise investor researches not only a company but the industry in which it operates.

Other Approaches: Annual and Quarterly

All of the basic do-it-yourself rules apply to other approaches except how frequently you review your portfolio. With a less frequent review of the stock portfolio, some precision and timing is lost but too frequent review can cause too much trading. As a friend once remarked to me, "You can't make stock prices go up by looking at them every day." The point of review – whether it occurs daily, monthly, or annually – is not to watch stock prices go up (although that may be a pleasurable bonus) but to learn more about the companies in which you have invested and to research other potential investment candidates. It is easy to be mesmerized by the daily ups and downs of stock prices. To succeed, however, you must focus on the longer term prospects of each company.

An annual review is one possible approach. I recommend spending a full day reading all of the available material received through the year. Save the annual and quarterly reports, as well as any articles and research reports, for each company in which you've invested or are considering investment. A simple folder for each would suffice. At the end of the annual review, decide which investments to keep and which to sell. Also, assess the amount of each holding. You might want to reduce your holding of a company that hasn't met your expectations but still shows promise; you might wish to add to a solid investment by purchasing more shares. Ideally, schedule your annual review shortly after you receive most of your annual reports. Many companies operate on a calendar-year basis, with annual reports available three to four months after the year-end; given this, a date in May might be a good choice.

A quarterly review also has merit as an approach, since companies send shareholders quarterly reports of their activities. While quarterlies are much less informative than annuals, these reports do contain relevant data on earnings as well as significant corporate developments. If you choose this strategy, time your quarterly review to coincide with the receipt of these reports. After each careful assessment of your investment portfolio, decide what stocks to buy and trade, and then carry out your decisions.

Keep an Ideas File with information on potential new

investments. Drop into it any material you come across that suggests a good investment, and any notes you make from observing businesses and products in your daily life. One month in advance of your quarterly or annual review, go through the Ideas File and compile the information needed to aid your decision-making. You need to be careful that your new investment ideas are still current and not rooted in eleven-month-old clippings. News travels instantly in our networked world; get the latest information on a company before investing.

These less frequent review approaches have the advantage of encouraging you to hold investments for a longer period of time. Patience is built into the approach. You are protected against falling victim to the addiction of daily trading that's based on whim or minor news, and you have a better chance of catching big trends and riding them profitably.

One caution: the thirty-minutes-per-day approach has a large learning component to it, dedicated, as it is, to researching individual companies and understanding the art of investing. A less frequent approach will necessarily diminish the pace at which you learn.

Seven Rules of Investment Tradecraft

1. Build a library
2. Generate investment ideas
3. Do your homework
4. Set clear objectives
5. Monitor your portfolio
6. Trust yourself
7. Have fun!

1. Build a Library

Assemble key books and gain access to a good flow of current information. Among the books I recommend for basic background: *Beating the Street* by Peter Lynch and John Rothschild, *Gordon Pape's 2004 Buyer's Guide to RRSPs* by Gordon

Pape, and *The Wealthy Barber* by David Chilton. Read them carefully.

For up-to-date information, I recommend daily *The Globe and Mail's Report on Business* and the *National Post's Financial Post* section. These two publications cover Canadian markets very well. If you are on a low budget, these newspapers are readily attainable in public libraries or online through your library card. Further suggestions for helpful reading material are in the Reading List the final section of this book.

Watch for articles not just on the companies in which you have an interest, but on the industries in general. Also, keep in mind the importance of staying informed about demographics and other trends. Changes in the overall age of the population will affect the fortunes of many products or services – retirement homes or movie theatres may be a better bet than Toys "R" Us! Similarly, long-term trends in prices, employment, and other economic factors can affect some kinds of business more than others. The smart investor stays well informed.

2. Generate Investment Ideas

As Peter Lynch points out in *Beating the Street*, within our daily lives is an array of investment possibilities: where you work, shop and live may provide leads to companies worthy of pursuit. As noted earlier, some of my best investment leads have come from friends, from observing the world around me, from encountering companies on business, and even from drinking beer in China.

Many of Peter Lynch's best ideas came from similarly ordinary activities, such as visits to the mall or observations on how the home mortgage market worked in the United States. What products are you buying for your children? What trends are there in your neighbourhood? Which companies seem to be doing a quality job?

Finding a good product or service in the marketplace is often a place to start, but it does not mean you should rush out and buy stock in its company. You need to amass all of the information that you can on the company and its stock, and determine whether or not the company fully reflects the value you see in it (more on this below). Nevertheless, remember that your investing experience takes place within the context of your life experience. A ski vacation in Whistler led to my son's interested in Intra-West, a company that has done a spectacular job of restoring Mont-Tremblant, Quebec, as a tourist destination by pioneering multiple major ski resorts in the city. It has turned out to be a solid investment based on a positive life experience.

The key is to find your leads, and do your Sherlock Holmes routine before you buy.

3. Do Your Homework

Your first step as a sleuth is to obtain as much information as possible about the companies you are investigating. Begin with the company itself, starting with their annual report.

The annual corporate report is an essential investment tool. At the end of each fiscal year, corporations report on their financial progress and their operations. As well, most corporations produce interim reports each quarter. These reports are easy to obtain and provide significant insight into the heath, prosperity, and even future prospects of a company.

There are several methods of obtaining annual reports. The most straightforward method is to simply write or email the company in which you are interested: address your request to the corporate secretary. Include your mailing address, and ask to be sent the most recent annual report, as well as to be added to the quarterly and annual report mailing list. (An added advantage to getting on the company's mailing list is that regular receipt of reports will remind you to stay on top of your investment!). As you become a more sophisticated investor, you may also want to request the corporation's Form 10-K report. This report, which the U.S. Securities and Exchange Commission requires companies to submit, includes details about executive compensation and other matters.

There are also annual reports services, which have the advantage of allowing you to obtain many annual reports at once. In Canada, *The Globe and Mail* offers a free Annual Reports Service which you can access under Resources at www. globeinvestor.com — there are approximately 400 annual reports available here. Similarly, if you are interested in U.K. or global companies, the *Financial Times* of London has its own service you can access at www.ftannualreports.com.

Many companies are now making their annual and quarterly reports available online through these services. This is an excellent means of obtaining information quickly. Corporate websites can also provide additional information such as up-to-date news releases.

Once you get your hands on these annual reports, it's time to read them. The next section will give you some guidelines regarding what to look for as you read. I have tried to make it a rule never to invest in a corporation until after reading its most recent annual report. I haven't had sufficient discipline to hold myself to this rule in each and every instance – to my regret. Some of my investing mistakes would have been avoided if I had possessed the patience to wait for, and undertake careful scrutiny of, the annual report.

Reading Annual Reports

An annual report may seem intimidating at first, but with a little practice, you can learn to find all kinds of useful information. Ask yourself: how well is the company doing? Why? Does it expect to do better in coming years? Does it have a lot of debt? How much debt and at what interest rate? Is it involved in any litigation, and if so, why? What are the sources and uses of the company's cash flow? Is the company producing cash flow from its operations, or is it borrowing money to meet its investment needs? As you read the report, pay particular attention to the disclosure of unusual items. These disturbing or pleasant surprises are tucked away in the notes that accompany the financial statement — scrutinize these notes. Another important section to read closely is the Management's Discussion and Analysis.

Besides reading the report with an eye for unusual information, good or bad, you will want to check out the financial statements of a corporation, which includes several sections that are essential to the investor:

- Income Statement
- Return on Equity
- Balance Sheet
- Cash Flow Statement (also called Statement of Changes in Financial Position).

You don't need to be an accountant to read the vital signs. Common sense and basic arithmetic will take you far. A calculator is all the tech help you need. The key elements to look for within each of these sections are discussed below.

Income Statement

The most important piece of information on the income statement is whether or not the company earned a profit. You should also check out how the company fared in the marketplace as measured by revenue; compare this figure to the year before, and to sales. Finally, the cash flow figure – literally, the amount of cash that "flowed" through the company – will add to your picture of a firm's financial health.

Return on Equity

Equity is the investor's real stake in the company. The return on shareholders' equity is what the company is earning for you, the shareholder. It is, therefore, a key piece of information to look for in annual reports. To assess how good the news actually is, compare the rate of return to that of previous years as well as to other companies in the same industry. To calculate return on equity, divide net earnings by shareholders' equity. These explorations will reveal whether or not a company is growing and remaining profitable.

Balance Sheet

A third important indicator of a company's status is its balance sheet. This statement is not mysterious; it simply records the assets and liabilities of the company. For an investor, the important questions that the balance sheet answers are:

- Did assets increase? If so, how do the increases in assets compare to increases in debt?
- How much debt is the company carrying? The less debt, the stronger the balance sheet.

Cash Flow Statement

The importance of total cash flow, which appears on the income statement, was mentioned above. Financial reports also include a Cash Flow Statement, or Statement of Changes in Financial Position, which records three clusters of activity: operating, investing, and financing activities. These categories capture, respectively, the business operation, the acquisition or sale of assets, and capital raised for the business. You are looking for a business that is growing, buying assets, and raising capital so that it does not become overburdened with debt.

Reading Annual Reports for Value

Not all reports are equally valuable. Some corporations choose to fully disclose their situations, including all risks as well as all potential. Others meet only the minimum standards necessary for disclosure in an annual report and concentrate on making their prospects look as good as possible. Over the years, there's been a trend towards greater disclosure in annual reports, partly because reporting requirements have strengthened, and partly because of voluntary corporate efforts. Nevertheless, when you read a company's report, especially for the first time, it's worth considering the quality of the earnings. The income statement tells you the amount the company earned, but you may have to read further to discover the real value behind this figure. Did these earnings come from their continuing operations — that is, the business in which the company intends to continue — or were they the result of a one-time event? Often, a corporation will sell an asset or investment in another corporation and record a large one-time profit. If you buy shares in a corporation expecting these types of profits to continue, you will be disappointed.

It is also worth delving into the arcane subject of how the corporation accounts for earnings. Some corporations have been known to inflate their earnings by recording all revenue at the time of sale. The more conservative approach is to record revenue as the activity proceeds. Different approaches to accounting — aggressive versus cautious — can have a profound impact on the quality of the corporation's reported earnings. Read the Management's Discussion and Analysis to get an idea of how a given company does things. Do managers feel that earnings will continue to grow? Are there one-time items? Are there reasons for caution?

As an investor, you should think of corporate annual reports as a key part of your strategy. Careful, thoughtful reading of an annual report is much more important than following the daily fluctuations of a stock price, yet many people spend their time trying to read deep meaning into stock shifts of a few cents and ignore the wealth of information coming through their mailboxes. Long-term trends for any corporation are based on success in the marketplace. It is the success of the business enterprise that ultimately generates value for shareholders. Acquiring and reading annual reports is a big first step in understanding the business upon which your investment prosperity depends.

Other Sources of Information

Besides the all-important annual reports (and their quarterly siblings), corporations often supply other kinds of information that are of interest to an investor.

Companies of all sizes send out press releases to business media outlets whenever a major event occurs in the corporation. Usually, you can get on the press release mailing list just by asking. When you send in your request to get on a company's annual report list, also inquire about access to press releases. This way, you will be kept up to date whether or not the news media actually pick up the story.

Corporations also release circulars prior to annual general meetings. These circulars provide information regarding executive compensation, which can be useful. How is senior management rewarded? Are there incentives to outperform the market? Are management rewarded with share options for increasing the share price value? If you are a shareholder, you are entitled to receive a copy of the annual; it's included in your initiation to the annual shareholders' meeting. If you are merely an interested party considering an investment, you may be able to request a copy. And in most cases, observers are welcome to attend annual general meetings.

When you are considering investing in a company, it's worth finding out if recent recommendations have been made about its stock by any professional investment analysts. *Investor's Digest of Canada* provides analyst estimates of many stock earnings for the current and upcoming year, as well as the names of brokerage firms that are following those stocks. *Investor's Digest* is available in most libraries, on newsstands, and by subscription.

It is possible – likely even, if you have discovered an especially undervalued stock – that the firms in which you are interested have not been covered by analysts. In these cases, you are on your own. And if you do find reports on a stock that interests you, remember that analysts often exhibit herd behaviour: they tend to have similar opinions, and by the time these opinions are published, the stock in question may no longer be a hidden gem. Nevertheless, an expert analysis can be a good way of testing your own judgment. And, if you invest in an analyst-recommended stock and you are wrong, at least you are wrong in distinguished, professional company!

Finally, the internet abounds with information on every subject, and investing is no exception. Besides corporate websites, which, as mentioned above, often provide annual reports and current news releases, there are numerous websites that provide company information and tools for analyzing stocks. Most are free, although some charge for special services. A few of the better online sources are:

- *Stock-Tools*, which lists 36,000 companies, at: www.stock-tools.com
- *Yahoo Finance*, an excellent site with the ability to allow you to set up your own online portfolios. Once set up, these portfolios automatically attract all news about companies included. This is a very powerful information and research tool.
- *The Motley Fool* at fool.com

Examining Your Reasoning

The final step in your pre-stock purchase homework is to identify your three best reasons for buying the stock. Are you influenced by the industry, the company prospects, or some hidden assets? Additionally, you'll want to determine the three biggest risks, so that you can monitor them. What would cause you to sell this stock? What is your price target? If, for example, you were to buy the stock at $5, do you hope to sell it at $6, $10, or $20? Is this stock purchase based on the belief that lower interest rates will continue? That high prices for natural gas will continue? You need to be honest with yourself about what would cause you to change your view, and you need to monitor those factors on a daily basis. You want to avoid overreacting to minor moves in the market, and ensure that your initial rationale behind the purchase still holds true.

4. Set Clear Objectives

As with most endeavours, your investing efforts will benefit from goal-setting. In these times of low inflation, an investment target of 12-15% of the total portfolio is reasonable. If inflation increases, you may want to move to the higher end of this range.

Your risk tolerance will also affect your goal. This will depend on your age, financial circumstances, and personality. The magic of compound interest is often used to illustrate the virtues of long-term investing; small contributions grow large portfolios over the long haul due to "interest on interest." If your tolerance for risk is low, you will want to concentrate on safer investments, and must be willing to accept the often lower returns these bring in exchange for security. If, however, you are willing to shoulder a little more risk, you have the opportunity for more significant returns.

5. Monitor Your Portfolio

Once your homework is done, you're ready to place your order. You should place it at a fixed price. Be certain to follow up to make sure your purchase has been made. You may need to raise the price. In my experience, Monday is a good day to buy stocks, as markets are often soft. Apparently, weekends inspire pessimism in investors. When it comes time to sell, choose another day.

Selecting and buying stocks, however, is only half the battle. You need to take an active role in ensuring that your overall portfolio is performing effectively. This will mean periodically weeding the garden to remove those stocks that, because something has changed in their operating environments, have not met your expectations. And of course, it may also mean selling stocks that have exceeded your expectations and become overpriced in the marketplace. There will also be stocks that remain in your portfolio for a very long time. If you find a company that you believe has a bright future and it continues to perform solidly, you may want to stick with it as a core holding. But it is only through continued attention that you'll be able to decide which stocks fall into which category.

Your custodian, usually a bank, will send you a monthly

statement listing your portfolio. Generally, these statements include each stock's market value — the price times the number of shares for each holding — and sometimes, cost value, which is the amount you paid to purchase. Keep these statements in a binder and refer to them during your daily strategy sessions. Remind yourself of why you own these positions and ask yourself what might cause you to exit a particular company or industry. It is worth engaging in a formal review, both quarterly and annually: look at everything in your portfolio and decide what should stay, what should go, and in some cases, what positions should be increased. Take a lesson from my mistakes: don't be impatient. Don't hesitate to sell a poorly performing stock, but be sure you are selling for a good reason. Sometimes, an initial investment in a company will lead you to gain faith in its future, and buy more.

Buying Small

You will also want to monitor stocks you are considering for investment. One tactic I have successfully employed over the years is to acquire a small holding in a company in which there is potential. The rationale supporting the purchase of a small shareholding is twofold. First, it taps you into the company's information flow, as you receive the annual and quarterly reports, and, if you ask, the press releases. Second, it allows you to compare the stock to others in your portfolio and better assess whether or not to add to the holding. Owning a few hundred shares — or in some cases, just one share — in a company, is a good way to force yourself to get an education in its affairs.

The Canadian Shareowners Investment Inc and DRIPs

Another technique for low-cost investing that simultaneously allows you to monitor a number of companies, is to join the Canadian Shareowners Investments Inc. Through this organization, you can purchase an initial single share of a number of corporations and enroll in a dividend reinvestment program (DRIP). Membership has the advantage of allowing you, with very little money invested, to gain ownership in, and knowledge of, a series of companies. When it comes to distribution of information, companies do not distinguish between their smallest and largest shareholder. Although it is unlikely that you'll be asked to join its board of directors if you only own a few shares, you will receive timely mailings of all relevant material and you will, over time, come to know the company.

Knowledge is power when it comes to investing. Knowing more than the average investor about a company can help you avoid error; it can enable you to forecast potential ahead of the market. Knowing that the oil drilling companies lacked debt led me to invest more aggressively, and ultimately, benefit more from my investments. You, too, can profit by knowing more about the companies to which you entrust your money.

The other benefit to many DRIPs is that you are spared the commission fee usually charged on market transactions. Many companies in Canada and the United States offer DRIPs. In Canada, these include BCE, Terasen Gas (formerly BC Gas), World National Bank, Bruncor, Canadian General Investments, Imperial Oil, and many others. Most companies with DRIPs cover all administrative expenses. In addition, some companies offer a 5% discount on reinvested dividends. Over a period of time, dividend reinvestment can allow you to amass, without significant cost, a larger holding in a company. While it is not a good idea to purchase shares in a company simply because they offer a DRIP, it is worth knowing whether or not a company in which you plan to invest offers this feature.

The Canadian Shareowners Investment Inc can be reached at:
4 King Street West, Suite 806
Toronto, Ontario M5M 1B6
Telephone – (416) 995-7200
Fax – (416) 595-0400
Email: customercare@shareowner.com

6. Trust Yourself

None of the advice in this book will be of benefit unless you have the courage to take some risks and, above all, are willing to learn from your mistakes. Investing can be both an entertaining hobby and a productive and profitable method of securing a better retirement income. But you need to know whether or not you can juggle the demons of fear and greed and keep your balance. You need, in the words of Rudyard Kipling, to "keep your head when all about you are losing theirs." You need to have your own views and not be swayed by panics in the market. That is not to say you should ignore the overall market, but you should have your own view of events and their potential. You will be investing in companies, not the market. Remember that a contrarian approach — buying when others are selling — can lead to big gains. And when you are sure of your faith in a stock, don't be timid — buy big. This approach will require boldness. Fortunately, you don't need to plunge in headfirst. You can begin by dipping a toe into the investment waters and seeing how you do.

Remember the motto in gunnery. Most people presume that the artillery commander's orders are, "Ready, aim, fire." This is not, in fact, the case. The dictum for artillery gunners is, "Ready, fire, aim." In gunnery, you isolate the target by firing first, and then assessing and adjusting your mark accordingly. This approach bodes well in investing. There is no perfect strategy; there are no perfect tips. Markets are volatile. The only way to succeed is to make some choices, and then learn from them. As legendary hockey player Wayne Gretzky has pointed out, "You miss 100% of the shots you don't take."

7. Have Fun!

A final word from my insightful Dutch friend, Dr. Okma: "It is serious business, but do not let it take over your life. After all, you also need to spend the money!" Occasionally, I pass by a brokerage office in a mall and see a crowd of people watching the ticker tape roll by. I imagine there are many more who watch it scroll across their television screens. These people have the same hungry look of those spectators desperately clutching their betting stubs at horse races. The difference is that horse races have a beginning, middle, and end. You place your bets, and then collect your winnings or tear up your ticket. The stock market is not a horse race. Do not become a spectator or a gambler. Become a thoughtful student of investing.

14 Getting Professional Help

Canadian-Focused Mutual Funds

If the do-it-yourself approach is not for you, another interesting route is the Canadian-focused mutual fund. A mutual fund is a group or pool of investments – generally stocks or bonds – in which you purchase units. If the fund includes 300 different stocks, then each unit consists of a tiny piece of each of the 300 companies. Mutual funds are handled by professional managers. Mutual fund units can be bought and sold daily, or sometimes weekly; prices fluctuate in accordance with changes in the prices of the stocks that the fund owns. Some mutual funds specialize in one industry, such as utilities or healthcare; others specialize in a geographic region, such as Poland or China or Canada; still others are general, and invest wherever gains seem likely. As with individual investments in stocks or bonds, the investor has the benefit of liquidity – the ability to cash in quickly. Sometimes there are fees for buying and selling mutual funds, which discourage investors from shifting from one fund to another. Often, the larger mutual fund companies — those that manage dozens of funds themselves — allow movement between funds without penalties. There are many mutual funds that focus exclusively on Canadian equities.

In Canada, today, there are some 1,800 mutual funds – slightly more than the 1,500 companies listed on the Toronto Stock Exchange. Which one to choose? How to select the right fund?

Numerous books are devoted purely to mutual fund ratings. Frequently, financial magazines and newspapers publish performance statistics on mutual funds. These sources of information have two problems. First, all the published data is about past performance, which is not a guarantee of future performance. Second, managers move from fund to fund. Superstars — such as Peter Lynch, who built the Fidelity Magellan fund to a top performer — depart, and are replaced by newcomers without proven records. Furthermore, the performance of a mutual fund is only properly judged over a three-, five-, or even ten-year period. Like any other investor, a mutual fund manager will need time to achieve value on a particular investment. However, if a fund consistently underperforms against its competitors, it is time to shift to another fund.

A strong mutual fund "family" is important as it allows you to move your assets from one fund to another without penalty. So if, for example, emerging markets seem ahead of their real values, a single phone call can switch your RESP back into a safe T-bill or money market fund. Even the most well-informed investor with a small portfolio is unlikely to assemble a successful diversified global portfolio. For global markets, and particularly in emerging markets, the expertise of a mutual fund manager important.

At Lawrence Decter Investment Counsel Inc, we manage three mutual funds; the Redwood Diversified Equity Fund and the Redwood Diversified Income Fund and most recently, the newly launched Redwood Global Small Cap Fund.

Redwood Diversified Equity Fund (RAM 201)

The investment objective of the Redwood Equity Diversified Fund is to provide long-term capital appreciation with potential for income by investing primarily in Canadian equity investments, income trusts, fixed-income investments and other Canadian income-producing securities.

Redwood Diversified Equity Fund Historical Performance to Dec 30, 2007

Fund Performance			Benchmarks		
Year	YTD	Inception (10/04)	S&P/TSX YTD	Universe Bond YTD	80/20 Blend YTD
2007	17.05%	19.41%	7.07%	3.50%	6.36%
2006	20.16%	20.13%	14.5%	4.06%	12.41%
2005	19.91%	20.08%	21.91%	6.46%	18.82%

Top Ten Holdings listed alphabetically (at Dec 31, 2007)

- Brookfield Asset Management Prefund
- CAE Inc
- Franco-Nevada Corp
- HudBay Minerals
- Monsanto Company
- Petrobank Energy
- PotashCorp
- Rocky Mountain Dealerships Inc
- Verenex Energy Inc
- Straits Resources Ltd

Redwood Diversified Income Fund (RAM 202)

The investment objective of this fund is principally to provide a consistent stream of income with potential for capital appreciation by investing in Canadian income-producing securities and Canadian equities.

Redwood Diversified Income Fund Historical Performance to Dec 30, 2007

Fund Performance			Benchmarks		
Year	YTD	Inception (10/04)	S&P/TSX YTD	Universe Bond YTD	80/20 Blend YTD
2007	11.03%	14.07%	7.07%	3.50%	6.36%
2006	8.00%	13.88%	14.5%	4.06%	12.41%
2005	16.52%	19.04%	21.91%	6.46%	18.82%

*Performance inclusive of distribution fees

Top Ten Holdings listed alphabetically (at Mar 28, 2008)

- Armtec Infrastructive Income Fund
- CAE Inc
- Franco-Nevada Corp
- Kinross Gold Corporation
- Inter Pipeline Fund
- Petrobank Energy
- Monsanto Company
- Tim Hortons Inc
- Venerex Energy Inc
- PotashCorp

These two mutual funds have performed well over the last three years, but there are many other excellent funds from which to choose. Our advice is to consider smaller mutual funds focused on Canada. Some of the larger funds are constrained in their performance by the size of the Canadian equity market.

Find a Trusted Investment Advisor

The image of the trusted advisor or broker looms large in television advertisements for financial products; a wise father-in-law or solid business colleague is always urging us to choose a particular brokerage house or mutual fund outfit. This image is misleading. Your trusted advisor may not have white hair, may be thirty years of age versus sixty, and may be female. The only necessary characteristic that your trusted advisor must possess is knowledge of investments. To work effectively with an investment advisor, you need to be able to communicate well and you must feel confident that you are getting solid advice. Don't be bashful about meeting with more than one investment advisor before you make your decision. You also need to be very honest about your risk tolerance and your time frame. If you can't sleep at night because your portfolio is in highly volatile stocks, you have too much risk. If you are disappointed by small returns year after year, you may have too little risk. Good questions to ask potential investment advisors include: What are your 3-, 4- and 10-year returns? What would you recommend for my portfolio? Requesting references s is also a good idea.

Find an Investment Counsel Firm

The difference between an investment advisor (often called a broker), and an investment counsel firm, is discretion. The investment advisor requires that the client make the final decision, while investment counsel firms manage accounts on a discretionary basis — you set your objective and risk tolerance, and the investment counsellor chooses your portfolio and makes decisions within it accordingly.

As noted earlier, with the help of a team of nine dedicated and talented staff, I manage an investment counsel firm, Lawrence Decter Investment Counsel Inc. We manage over $400 million for our clients. There are several dozen other such firms, some larger, some smaller. Depending on the size of your portfolio and your objectives, an investment counsel firm may be the way to go. Many of the larger firms have a minimum account size of $1-$2 million. Our own firm has a minimum of $250,000. Clearly, investment counselling is not for those with very small accounts to invest. But it is an alternative for those with significant funds who do not want the burden of doing it themselves.

15 RRSPs

Whichever approach to investing you choose, a Registered Retired Savings Plan (RRSP) is a very good vehicle.

RRSPs were introduced in the 1957 federal budget. The principle behind them is simple: until the money deposited into an RRSP is withdrawn, its taxation is deferred. By age 71, you are required to convert your RRSP into a Registered Retirement Income Fund (RRIF) and begin gradual withdrawals. The government created this sheltered investment avenue to encourage individual Canadians to save for retirement. RRSPs are highly attractive vehicles for saving money: contributions are deductible from taxable income up to certain maximums; the interest, dividends, and capital gains on monies invested are not taxable until withdrawn; when the money is withdrawn, the rate of taxation is determined by your income at the time of the withdrawal — which usually occurs in retirement. An RRSP effectively transfers money earned during high-income years to our later, low-income years, giving Canadians who do not belong to a company pension plan similar access. And in the meantime, RRSP funds, like pension funds, can be put to work for you.

RRSPs

Until the mid-1960s, RRSP investment was slow, with only insurance companies involved as plan administrators. In the late 1960s, the mutual fund industry began to offer RRSP investments, and by the mid-1970s, the banks joined, raising the RRSP investment in Canada from $27 million in 1960 to $4 billion in 1980. Over the last thirty years, there has been active competition to sell these financial products.

For many Canadians, after home ownership and company pension plan, an RRSP represents their largest single investment. For an increasing number of young Canadians who rent and do not have a company pension plan, an RRSP is their only major investment. And yet, according to a 2005 Statistics Canada report, only 58% of Canadian families had an RRSP. For those between the ages of 45-54, that increases to 68%, and from 55-64, to 69%. Still, almost half of the Canadian population had not taken advantage of this opportunity to save and invest.

The choices for RRSP holdings in Canada are broader than most people realize. Most Canadians hold term deposits, bonds, or mutual funds in their RRSPs. But you can also use RRSPs to hold individual stocks that are traded on stock exchanges. Home mortgages are also eligible investments although administrative costs are high. You can construct your own investment portfolio of individual stocks and other financial assets. It is even possible to hold shares in a privately-owned business through an RRSP, although the rules for this are complex and legal advice is required.

To make sound decisions about your RRSP, you need to understand the laws and regulations that govern it. You do not need to become a legal scholar; some simple basics will suffice. The key concept is that your RRSP is like a pension fund. You pay no tax on the earnings while the money is working for you in the portfolio. Tax is deferred until you withdraw your funds for retirement.

The magic of tax-free compounding and investment success combine to make RRSPs the most important savings opportunity available to you. The tax deductibility of your contributions, up to a defined limit, is also extremely valuable. The painful reality that employers and governments are not looking out for everyone's eventual retirement is only gradually dawning upon many Canadians. The government has provided an attractive framework for saving, but you must take responsibility for making it work.

The RRSP offers individuals significant opportunity. Is it a risky social policy? The values of a society are reflected in how it supports the most vulnerable of its citizens. The darker side of the RRSP opportunity is the loss of interest by the Canadian middle class in the continued success of the Canada Pension Plan (CPP). As RRSPs replace the CPP as a major source of retirement savings, support for a strong CPP is dwindling. As the CPP erodes, the pension safety net that protects our less well-off citizens in their retirement years will have less public and political support. The problem is not only harmful to those who depend on the CPP — it also throws a burden on governments, and therefore, on all of us. As citizens we may have this concern. As individuals who will eventually need retirement income, we need to build our own savings via RRSPs.

Those who are able and willing to invest in RRSPs will have more prosperous retirements. Others will be disadvantaged, some by poor planning, but many others simply by their financial circumstances. Social policy should ensure a decent retirement income for all Canadians. To accomplish this, Canada needs to keep the CPP strong, well-funded, and properly invested. RRSPs should be a supplement for those able and willing to save beyond the CPP, not a substitute for missing or inadequate pension plans.

To be secure, your retirement income should rest on three pillars. First, whatever is left of the CPP — likely no more than a modest base. Second, your employer pension plan, if you have one. Third is your RRSP-based retirement income. This is the pillar over which you have control, and can strengthen.

How to Maximize Your RRSP Value

The best strategy for maximizing the value of your RRSP is careful, thoughtful investment. However, there are also tactics that can help your RRSP grow faster than it otherwise might. To fully take advantage of the possibilities, it's important that you familiarize yourself with the RRSP rules and regulations. And, because rules often change with each federal budget, you'll want to follow post-budget press coverage for any new wrinkles. Although contributions to RRSPs are significant, they fall well short of the maximum that the law allows. Statistics Canada estimated that in 2006, total unused "contribution room" reached over $437 billion of eligibility for all Canadians. Your concern is not the total but your own situation. Do you have room to add to your RRSP?

The maximum amount you can contribute is reduced by any pension contributions made at your place of employment. Your pension adjustment (PA) reflects any benefits from an employer-sponsored RRSP. In order to find out how much you can contribute, deduct your PA from 18% of your income.

RRSP Rules as of 2008

Deadline for Contributions:	For a given tax year, March 1 of the following year.
Contribution Limit:	Lesser of $19,000 or 18% of earned income for previous year; $20,000 for 2008; and $21,000 for 2009.
Earned income Includes:	Employment income (less dues and expenses); disability payments from Canada or Quebec Pension Plan; net rental income; net research grants received;

supplementary unemployment benefit plan payments received (not Employment Insurance); net business income; net royalties received; net alimony or separation allowance received; employee profit-sharing plan allocations.

Earned Income Excludes: Interest; dividends; capital gains; pension income.

Carry-forward: As of 1991, any unused "contribution room" can be carried forward indefinitely.

Over-contribution: There is a lifetime over-contribution of $2,000 allowed. Over-contributions in excess of this amount are subject to a 1% per month penalty tax. The $2,000 is a cumulative amount, not an annual allowable figure, and applies whether or not the contribution was made to a spousal plan. Over-contributions are not allowable for plan holders under the age of 18.

Spousal Plan: Contributions to an RRSP for a spouse are permitted. Special rules for contributions and withdrawals.

Home Buyers' Plan: Plan holders may withdraw up to $20,000 if they qualify as a first-time home buyer. RRSP contributions that are withdrawn within ninety days of deposit are not deductible.

Source: Developed from material on Canadian Revenue Agency website www.cra-arc.gc.ca

Contributing Early — For Maximum Compound Growth

Most Canadians start working in their early twenties but don't start contributing to RRSPs until they are, on average, age 34. Early-year RRSP contributions have much more time to grow in value. And the financial impact of contributing more money is significant. A calculation by *SmartMoney* magazine showed that a contribution of $200 per month grew to $175,000 over seventeen years at 8% per annum. If an extra $100 per month was contributed, the total grew to $225,000 over the same seventeen years. That extra $100 was worth an additional $50,000.

The power of compound growth is great. At 15%, my target annual rate for my investment, $1 becomes $3 in ten years, $9 in twenty years, and $34 in thirty-two years. Even at 10% per year, your portfolio will double in seven years. The advantages of investing early cannot be overstated!

The other way in which you can contribute early is to put your year's contribution into your RRSP at the beginning of the year. Many Canadians wait until the last minute — the RRSP deadline in a given tax year. This is an expensive tactic. You lose the benefit of earnings during the year and you may make bad investment choices in the end of RRSP season rush. Contributing as early as you can each year is a very effective way to increase growth.

Use Previous "Contribution Room"

If you do not contribute the allowable maximum to your RRSP in one year, you can carry the leftover amount forward to another. Under current rules, "contribution room" can be carried forward from 1991 on. You will need to complete some tax forms to access your old "contribution room," but this extra work is well worth the effort. It could allow you to shelter many thousands of additional savings and grow them without tax until retirement.

Minimize Your Fees

Check carefully to ensure you are not paying extra fees. Comparison shop! Most banks and discount brokers will waive the $100 annual administrative fee if you push. Not everyone charges it.

Consolidate Your Holdings

When you've signed up with a discount brokerage service or broker, consolidate your existing RRSP assets into this new account. However, if your RRSP is currently in term deposits at favourable rates of interest, you may want to wait and make the transfer after these term deposits expire. If you have extremely small RRSP assets and your financial institution charges a fee for transferring, you may want to simply leave your RRSP assets where they are and start your investment plan with your new contribution. Be careful that you don't lose a significant percentage, say 5-10%, of your funds in the transition.

Whichever approach you choose, remember that your RRSP can be a very powerful vehicle for growing your portfolio. The tax advantages are significant. Take your RRSP seriously as a terrific investment opportunity to manage your own investments.

16 Risks and Rewards

One of the truest of proverbs, originally penned by Voltaire, is that the best is the enemy of the good. Thus far, my case for investing in Canada has taken a very positive approach. However, there are several real risks to Canada's continuing prosperity that investors should, in prudence, take seriously. These include: the potential for profound decline in the American economy, the heightened value of the Canadian currency, the possibility of Quebec separating from Canada, and the chances of a cataclysmic event that sharply reduces the growth prospects of Asia, such as the Avian flu. These four risks are potential dark linings to the silver clouds that dominate Canada's investment prospects.

The Risk of an American Recession

A real risk to continuing growth of the North American economy is the banking liquidity crisis brought on by the sub-prime mortgage debacle in the United States. Although Canada's banks are sound, our economy is not immune to impacts from recession in the United States. If the U.S. goes into a major recession in the next five years, it could dramatically impact demand for some Canadian goods, particularly manufactured goods that are cost competitive in the U.S. but not in the rest of the world, particularly the developed world. The saying goes that if the U.S. sneezes, Canada catches cold. But not all Canadian exports to the U.S. are equally susceptible to changes in American conditions. In particular, exports of energy, oil and natural gas to the U.S. are somewhat less influenced by U.S. economic growth. Even if you're out of a job, you still have to heat your home or apartment.

According to the Government of Canada, over 87% of Canada's trade is with the United States. In 2006, total trade in goods and services reached $577 billion. Each day, 37,000 trucks rumble across the Canada-U.S, border transporting goods. This is the largest trading relationships in the world. Prime Minister Trudeau once commented that sharing the continent with the United States was not unlike "a mouse in bed with an elephant... no matter how friendly ... one is affected by every twitch and grunt." Canada's trade with the United States is an important part of Canadian prosperity. Many industries, such as the auto industry, are integrated across the border into a single, functioning manufacturing complex. The risk to these integrated manufacturing complexes comes largely from lower cost production in Asia, particularly China. Over the next five to ten years, it is likely that exports of automobiles and trucks will commence from China to the rest of the world. Just as the Chinese entry in the market brought down the cost of DVD players from $600 to $60, Chinese-produced automobiles and trucks could have a devastating affect on the Canadian and American auto industry. Both Ford and GM are currently struggling with serious financial difficulty. It seems less likely that one or both of GM and Ford will go into bankruptcy. Intriguingly, it is international sales that are keeping the so-called three big automakers afloat (including the Chrysler part of Daimler-Chrysler) while U.S. sales decline. Car sales in the Middle East, South America and even Africa, are growing for GM and Ford, and are generating much needed revenue.

Currency Risk

Canada's success has propelled the Canadian dollar back above par with the U.S. dollar, a level not seen in several decades. This high Canadian dollar means that Canadian exports to the U.S. are more expensive; American imports into Canada are less expensive. In short, the enormous trade surplus Canada has enjoyed is eroded by the increasing price of Canadian-manufactured goods. The high Canadian dollar is hurting Canadian exporters in all sectors. It is likely that the Bank of Canada will continue to cut Canadian interest rates with the goal of blunting the rise of the Canadian dollar.

The Risk of Quebec Separation

Since the 1960s, there has been active political pressure within the province of Quebec towards separatism. Organized political parties — the Parti Québécois (PQ) at the provincial level, and the Bloc Québécois (BQ), at the national level — are dedicated to achieving independence for Quebec. There have been two referendums, the most recent in 1995, wherein Quebecers have been asked whether or not they wish to negotiate separation from Canada. Both failed but the most recent referendum failed by a narrow margin. To date, the PQ has enjoyed political success governing the province of Quebec under Premiers René Lévesque, Jacques Parizeau and Bernard Landry. However, the PQ has not yet been able to mount a successful referendum appeal to achieve the conditions necessary to negotiate the exit of the province from Canada.

More troubling to those who would like to see Canada remain a single nation is the emergence of the BQ at the federal level. Over recent elections, the BQ has grown steadily in political power. In the 1993 election, they took a majority of Quebec seats in the House of Commons. There is a possibility that some time in the next decade there will be another referendum in Quebec and it is realistic to think that separatists might achieve a majority. Over the four or five decades of their active political involvement, separatists have commanded a hardcore base of 30-35% of the Quebec electorate. But the separatists occasionally catch a wave of popular, usually negative, sentiment, directed either against federalists in Quebec, or at Ottawa. Seen as remote from daily lives, the federal government is then blamed relentlessly by separatists for all problems that befall Quebec. In recent years, the fiscal gap or fiscal imbalance has been the argument advanced by Quebec. The fiscal imbalance thesis runs that the federal government is rich in revenue while the provinces are poor. Canada's Prime Minister Stephen Harper has pledged to address this issue: what he does may play a critical role in the matter of separation.

What consequences would Quebec's separation have on Canada's economic prospects? Those in favour of separation downplay the costs and risks, but it is certain that the negotiation would be ugly and difficult, and likely drag out for years or even decades, over issues such as the allocation of Canadian debt. Quebec separatists would also like to retain the Canadian dollar and remain part of the NAFTA in order to continue their access to U.S. markets. Much as most Canadians would like the country to stay together with Quebec as an important province, there is the risk of a breaking point. The discussion of constitutional issues in Canada and the debate over Quebec's role within the country have been described by former PQ leader Jacques Parizeau as "an endless trip to the dentist." It is possible that there would be a significant backlash from the rest of Canada in response to a positive referendum vote. Positions might harden and some amount of economic and governmental chaos might result. It is also likely that international investors would look askance at a divided Canada. Canada's good credit would be damaged and its currency devalued by the uncertainty of a positive referendum vote.

For investors, the separatist issue is not immediate, but it appears on the landscape from time to time as a potential risk to investing in Canada.

The Risk of an Asian Crisis

The fourth potential area of threat to Canadian business success and therefore, to opportunities for investors in Canada, is the possibility of a devastating event in Asia. Canada depends upon Asian markets for an increasing portion of our exports. In particular, the prices of copper, zinc, potash, grain and coal, and possibly uranium, have been buoyed by China's demand. Some pandemics — Avian flu, for example — could dramatically reduce economic growth in Asia, particularly China and India. This, in turn, could dramatically reduce demand for Canadian resources. To date, there's little hard evidence of an epidemic, despite the dire warnings of the World Health Organization. SARS, though not a major pandemic, provided a wake-up call for many public health agencies worldwide and caused Canada to establish the Public Health Agency of Canada. Canada is now much better organized to cope with the pandemic that may come our way. In summary, the risk of an Asian flu pandemic, while not to be ignored, should not deter investment in Canada.

How likely is Quebec separation, a major American recession or a global pandemic in the next five years? A U.S. recession is much more likely than Quebec separating. The Avian flu remains elusive. Clearly, any one of these three factors could pose a threat to investors in Canada; if two or three were to occur simultaneously, the results would be devastating.

The American economy sustained a blow to its main engine — consumer confidence. This blow came in the form of defaults on sub-prime mortgages. Much has been done by the Federal Reserve to lower interest rates, inject liquidity and intervene to stabilize the U.S. financial system. This will likely be enough to avoid a serious recession in the United States but not avert several quarters of very slow growth with attendant consequences for Canada.

Perils of a Stronger Canadian Dollar

The fourth factor, an increase in the value of the Canadian dollar, has already occurred. We are coping with both the benefits of greater purchasing power and the damage to Canadian manufacturing.

Canada's Century: At Last!

Prime Minister Wilfred Laurier's prediction that the 20th century would belong to Canada did not come true. Some would say Laurier exhibited political hubris. Perhaps he was just 100 years early, and Canada is the tortoise nation destined to win the long distance race against America.

The Mexicans have a lament stated by their former president Porfirio Diaz that reads, "So far from God and so close to the United States." There are certainly times and circumstances, such as the softwood lumber dispute, when Canadians might well share this lament. However, the American market, in all of its massive commercial glory, is a huge economic benefit to Canada. Our disputes, such as softwood lumber, affect less than 1% of our trade with the United States. The largest trading relationship between any two countries on the planet is relatively healthy. With the emergence of Asian and Indian markets and their need for Canadian resources and services, there is a real and growing second leg to Canadian trade success. We need to balance our efforts between the American market and growing markets of India and Asia. This second leg will also assist in blunting the impact of an American recession on Canadians.

If it can manage its internal divisions and solve its key issues, Canada is poised for an interesting and prosperous century. The world needs more Canada — and we should step up and provide more Canada; Canadian expertise, as well as Canadian resources, are needed in the developing world.

Customers in India and China want more than our oil and potash. They also want our talents: our engineering expertise and much more. In the competitive world of the 21st century, however, these customers will not beat a path to our door. We must build a bridge to meet their needs. Canada's success rests, in large measure, on our contribution to amending the needs of Asia's population. It is overwhelmingly in our interest to seize this opportunity. There is a diversity of investment opportunity in Canada. Invest in Canada —carefully — and prosper!

RESOURCES

READING LIST

Works Cited

Accounts of the United States, *Federal Reserve Flow of Funds*, Washington, June 2005

Bank of Canada website www.bank-banque-canada.ca

BMO Nesbitt Burns, *Provincial Government Finance*, February 2008

Canada.com website: www.canada.com/vancouversun/news/story/html

Canadian Institute for Health Information, *Health Care 2007*

Clayton Research Associates, Limited; Survey of Canadian Real Estate; February 2006

Coxe, Donald. *Basic Points-An Investment Journal*, BMO Nesbitt, Quarterly Publication, August, 2006

Department of Finance, Government of Canada, Federal Budget Department of Finance, Government of Canada, Plan for Growth and Prosperity, November 2005, Ottawa

Department of Finance, Government of Canada, *Surplus – Deficit – Fiscal Reference Tables*, September 2005, Ottawa

The Economist Magazine, *Pocket World in Figures*, 2008 Edition, Profile Books Ltd., London, U.K.

Energy Information Agency (EIA), *Accelerated Depletion: Accessing Its Impacts on Domestic Oil and Natural Gas Prices and Production*, Report RR/OIAK/2000-04

Foot, David K. *Boom, Bust & Echo: Profiting From the Demographic Shift in the 21st Century.* Toronto: Stoddart, 2001

Forbes Magazine, May 1997

Fortune 500 Study

Government of Canada. *A Plan for Prosperity and Growth*, 2005, Budget Federal Department of Finance, 2005.

Harrod, Roy. *The Life of John Maynard Keynes*. London, England: W.W. Norton & Company, 1983

Innis, Harold. *The Fur Trade in Canada.* Toronto: U of T Press Inc, 1930

Ministry of Finance, Government of Alberta, *Alberta Budgets 2003-2007*, Edmonton

OECD, *Economic Outlook*, No. 77, June 2005.

Oil Consumption by Country, www.nationmaster.com

Schulich, Seymour. *Get Smarter.* Toronto: Key Porter Books Ltd, 2007

Shell Oil, press release, April 20, 2006.

Statistics Canada, *Labour Force Survey 1970 – 1975: Labour Productivity*

Statistics Canada, *Registered Retirement Savings*; Canadian Holdings; 2005.

Statistics Canada, *The Alberta Juggernaut*, September 2006.

TD Bank. *Study of Natural Gas*, February, 2006.

Tertzakian, Peter. *A Thousand Barrels a Second: The Coming Oil Break Point and the Challenges Facing an Energy Dependant World.* New York: McGraw Hill, 2007

United Nations Survey of Crime Trends and Operations of Criminal Justice Systems (1998 – 2008); United Nations Office of Drug and Crime, Centre for International Crime Preventions.

World Bank, Lee Rapid (Schipper Wei-Shiuen Ng) *Motorization in China; Environmental and Social Challenges*, October 18, 2004.

World Nuclear Association website: www.worldnuclear.org

Corporate Annual Reports
- Advantage Energy Income Fund 2007
- Akita Drilling 1999 – 2007
- BP 2007
- Enerplus Resource Fund 2007
- Exxon 2007
- Franco-Nevada 2007
- Nortel 1998-2007
- Paramount Energy 2007

- Petrobank Energy and Resources Ltd 2006-07
- Peyto Energy 2007
- PotashCorp 2007
- Progress Energy 2007
- Royal Dutch Shell 2007
- TransCanada Corporation 1999-2007
- Trilogy Energy Trust 2007
- Vermilion Energy Trust 2007

Basic Investment Books

1. Chilton, David. *The Wealthy Barber.* Toronto: Stoddart, 1989.
   David Chilton's very sensible, easy-to-read guide has become a business all its own. With over a million copies in print, *The Wealthy Barber* has become a real classic – deservedly so. Buy it. Read it.

2. Decter, Michael B. *The DRIP Strategy: Building Your Wealth One Share at a Time With Dividend Investment Plans.* Toronto: Stoddart, 2001.
   This is the book for the micro investor who is just starting out. It describes the benefits of investing one share at a time and utilizing dividend reinvestment programs.

3. Decter, Michael B. *Million Dollar Strategy: Building Your Own Retirement Fund in Just Thirty Minutes a Day.* Toronto: Stoddart, 1998.
   The author's first book on investing. Focused on basic rules for investing and the benefits of RRSPs.

4. Farrel, Paul B. *Expert Investing on the Net: Profit From the Top-25 Online Money Makers.* New York: John Wiley & Sons, 1996.
   A great sourcebook for the field of internet investing.

5. Foot, David K. *Boom Bust & Echo: Profiting From the*

Demographic Shift in the 21st Century. Toronto: Stoddart, 2001.
Demographics, including the aging of the baby boom generation, will greatly influence markets.

6. Gardner, David and Gardner, Tom. *The Motley Fool Investment Guide: How the Fool Beats Wall Street's Wise Men and How You Can Too.* New York: Simon & Schuster, 1996.
An online investment duo puts it on paper.

7. Graja, Christopher and Ungar, Elizabeth. *Investing in Small-Cap Stocks.* New Jersey: Bloomberg Press, 1997.
A very systematic approach to investing in the small-cap sector.

8. Lewis, Michael. *Liar's Poker: Rising Through the Wreckage on Wall Street.* New York: W.W. Norton, 1989.
A fun read about life on Wall Street.

9. Lowenstein, Roger. *Buffett: The Making of an American Capitalist.* New York: Random House, 1995.
The story of America's greatest living investor, Warren Buffet is a must-read for fledgling and professional investors alike.

10. Lynch, Peter and Rothschild, John. *Beating the Street.* New York: Simon & Schuster, 1993. Making a case that the average investor has a good chance of beating the typical Mutual Fund manager over a sustained period.

11. Lynch, Peter and Rothschild, John. *One Up on Wall Street: How to Use What You Already Know to Make Money in the Market.* New York: Simon & Schuster, 2000.
The single best book to read on investing.

12. O'Shaughnessy, James P. *What Works on Wall Street.* New York: McGraw-Hill, 1996.
The other of the two best books on the list. A statistical look at how investment strategies stack up. A data-

based analysis that compares different strategies. This
book is worthwhile for the advanced reader.

13. Pape, Gordon. *Gordon Pape's 2004 Buyer's Guide to RRSPs.*
Toronto: Prentice-Hall, 1996.
A thorough review worth the investment. Includes
over 500 mutual funds.

14. Pape, Gordon. *Sleep Easy Investing.* Toronto: Penguin
Group Canada, 2008.

15. Templeton, Robert. *K.G. Paper Money.* New York: Summit
Books, Simon & Schuster, 1981.
A fun read. A great book on inflation and its impacts.

16. Woods, Shirley E. *Self-Directed RRSPs: Straight Talk on
Making Them Pay Off For You.* Toronto: John Wiley &
Son. 1997.
An excellent guide to those investments eligible for
RRSPs, with a great glossary.

TOP 50

Most of these companies have been mentioned in the text of the book. These are our top fifty long-term choices for investing in the Canadian economy. As with any investment, you must do your own homework and be careful with your timing.

Bank of Montreal (BMO)
Bank of Nova Scotia (BNS)
Boardwalk REIT (BEI.UN)
Brookfield Properties (BPO)
Cameco Corporation (CCO)
Canadian Imperial Bank of Commerce (CM)
Canadian National Railway (CNR)
Canadian Oil Sands (COS.UN)
Canadian Pacific Railway (CP)
Crescent Point (CPG.UN)
Denison Mines Corp (DML)
Duvernay (DDV)
Enbridge Inc (ENB)
EnCana (ECA)
Energy Savings Income Fund (SIF.UN)
First Service (FSV)
Fortis Inc (FTS)
Franco-Nevada Corporation (FNV)
Great-West Life (GWO)
HudBay Minerals Inc (HBM)
Imperial Oil (IMO)
Inter Pipeline Fund (IPL-UN)
Investors Group (IGM)
Keyera Facilities Income Fund (KEY.UN)
Manulife Financial Corporation (MFC)
New Flyer Industries (NFI.UN)
Pembina Pipelines Income Fund (PIF.UN)
Petrobank Energy and Resources (PBG)

PotashCorp (POT)
Power Corporation of Canada (POW)
Power Financial Corporation (PWF)
Research in Motion (RIM)
Rogers Communications (RCI.B)
Royal Bank (RY)
Savanna Energy Services Corp (SVY)
Shaw Communications (SJR.B)
Sherritt International Corp (S)
Shoppers Drug Mart Corporation (SC)
SNC-Lavalin Group Inc (SNC)
Suncor Energy Inc (SU)
Teck Cominco Limited (TCK.B)
Telus Corporation (T)
Teranet (TF.UN)
Tim Hortons (THI)
Toronto-Dominion Canada Trust (TD)
TransCanada Corp (TRP)
Verenex (VNX)
Vermilion Energy Trust (VET.UN)
Viterra (VT)
WestJet (WJA)

THE CANADIAN FUTURE 45

These are very small Canadian companies in their early stages. Some will fail and some will struggle. A few will be huge success stories. A few may have disappeared – already bought by others. Do not buy *any* of these equities without doing your own homework! Whenever possible, company websites are a valued asset to your research.

The Future 45:

ADF Group Inc (TSX: DRX), Market Cap: $111M
ADF Group Inc is a Quebec-based steel company that designs, engineers, fabricates and provides selective installation services for steel superstructures and architectural metal works throughout Canada and the United States.
www.adfgroup.com/index_flash.htm

Ag Growth Income Fund (TSX: AFN.UN), Market Cap: $423M
Ag Growth Income Fund is a construction, farm machinery and heavy trucks company. This company manufactures portable grain handling equipment including augers, belt conveyors and other grain handling accessories through 1,400 dealers and distributors in Canada and the United States.
www.aggrowth.com

Agtech Processors Inc (TSX: AGT.UN), Market Cap: $48M
Alliance Grain Traders Income Fund holds securities in Agtech Processors Inc, which acquires, processes and exports green lentils primarily to South America, North Africa and the Middle East. This company also operates food processing plants in Saskatchewan and North Dakota.

Anooraq Resources Corp (TSX: ARQ), Market Cap: $606M
Anooraq Resources Corp is a diversified metals and mining company which acquires, explores and develops prospective platinum group metals (PGM) properties. The company has projects in the Bushveld Complex in South Africa.
www.anooraqresources.com

Resources

Arise Technologies Corp (TSX: APV), Market Cap: $223M
Arise Technologies Corp is a solar technology company that provides a range of solar energy solutions, including solar energy design and consulting services and installation of custom solar energy solutions, primarily in Ontario.
www.arisetech.com/

Avcorp Industries Inc (TSX: AVP), Market Cap: $27M
Avcorp Industries Inc is an aerospace and defense company which supplies subcontract engineering design, manufactured parts, subassemblies and complex major assemblies for manufacturers of private and commercial civil aircraft.
www.avcorp.com

Axia NetMedia Corp (TSX: AXX), Market Cap: $191M
Axia NetMedia Corp is an internet services company that designs, builds, operates and develops high-performance real broadband open access networks that provide fragmented and under-served regions access to Internet Protocol (IP) connectivity.
www.axia.com

BioteQ Environmental Technologies Inc (TSX: BQE), Market Cap: $209M
BioteQ Environmental Technologies Inc is an environmental services company that developed and patented the Bio-Sulphide and ChemSulphide processes to treat metal-laden, sulphate-rich waste water streams for acid neutralization and metal recovery.
www.bioteq.ca

Blue Note Mining Inc (TSX: BN), Market Cap: $105M
Blue Note Mining Inc is a diversified metals and mining company which owns and operates the Restigouche lead-zinc mines located near Bathurst, New Brunswick.
www.bluenotemining.ca

Canoro Resources Ltd (TSX: CNS), Market Cap: $159M

Canoro is a Canadian-based international oil and gas company operating in the prolific Assam/Arakan basin of northeast India.

www.canoro.com

Cathay Forest Products Corp (TSX: CFZ), Market Cap: $78M

Cathay Forest Products Corp is a forest products company that manages standing timber properties and plants and harvests fast-growing poplar forest plantations in China and Russia.

www.cathayforest.com

Chariot Resources Ltd (TSX: CHD), Market Cap: $311M

Chariot Resources Ltd is a diversified metals and mining company that is developing its 70% owned Marcona copper project in Peru. This company is scheduled to be a mid-tier copper producer by 2009.

www.chariotresources.com

Cineplex Galaxy Income Fund (TSX: CGX.UN), Market Cap: $706M

Cineplex Galaxy owns and operates movie theatres across Canada.

www.cineplex.com

Discovery Air Inc (TSX: DA.A), Market Cap: $137M

Discovery Air Inc is an airline company which through three subsidiaries, operates air services, each with a fleet of aircraft, supported by aircraft maintenance bases throughout northern Canada.

www.discoveryair.com

Finavera Renewables (TSX: FVR), Market Cap: $58M

Finavera Renewables is dedicated to the development of renewable energy resources and technologies. This company is developing offshore power plants that produce renewable

electricity from wind and ocean wave energy in Ireland and Canada.
www.finavera.com

First Service Corp (TSX: FSV), Market Cap: $703M
First Service operates everything from College Pro Partners to managing 1500+ retirement communities in the United States. It is a diversified property services company.
www.firstservice.com

Formation Capital Corp (TSX: FCO), Market Cap: $117M
Formation Capital Corp is a diversifed metals and mining company that operates a precious metals refinery. It is developing a cobalt property in Idaho and holds mineral prospects in Saskatchewan and Mexico.
www.formcap.com

Gemcom (TSX: GCM), Market Cap: $144.3M
Gemcom provides software to the mining industry designed to automate and integrate key operations.
www.gemcomsoftware.com

Groupe Laperriere & Verreault Inc (TSX: LVG.A), Market Cap: $395
GLV Inc is a global provider of processes and technologies designed for various environmental, municipal and industrial applications. GLV's businesses are divided into two main groups: the water treatment group and the pulp and paper group.
www.glv.com

Isotechnika Inc (TSX: ISA), Market Cap: $137M
Isotechnika Inc is a biotechnology company that develops and plans to commercialize immunosuppressive therapeutic drugs for the treatment of autoimmune diseases and for use in the prevention of organ rejection in transplantation.
www.isotechnika.com

JAZZ Air Income Fund (TSX: JAZ.UN), Market Cap: $974M

Jazz Air Income Fund operates the Jazz airline under an agreement with Air Canada.
www.flyjazz.ca

Jite Technologies Inc (TSX: JTI), Market Cap: $50M

JITE Technologies Inc develops, manufactures and sells electronic terminal blocks used in security, elevator, railway and automation systems in North America and China.
www.jite.com

Kereco Energy Ltd (TSX: KCO), Market Cap: $234M

Kereco Energy Ltd is an oil and gas exploration and production company based in central and northwestern Alberta and northeastern British Colombia.
www.kereco.com

Kodiak Oil & Gas Corp (TSX: KOG), Market Cap: $294M

Kodiak Oil & Gas Corp is an oil and gas company exploring, developing and producing oil and natural gas in the U.S. Rocky Mountain region. Its core areas include the Vermillion Basin of the Greater Green River Basin and the Williston Basin in Montana and North Dakota.
www.kodiakog.com

Liberty Mines Inc (TSX: LBE), Market Cap: $184M

Liberty Mines Inc is a diversified metals and mining company that owns and operates the Redstone nickel mine in Timmins, Ontario and is developing the nearby McWatters nickel mine.
libertymines.com

Magindustries Corp (TSX: MAA), Market Cap: $543M

Magindustries Corp is developing magnesium, potash and eucalyptus forestry assets at Pointe Noire in the Kouilou region of the Republic of Congo and electrical generation assets in the Congo. *www.magindustries.com*

Resources

Migao Corp (TSX: MGO), Market Cap: $325M
Migao Corp manufactures specialty potash-based fertilizers at three facilities in China for the Chinese market. Primary products include potassium nitrate and potassium sulphate which are suited for high-value crops such as fruits and vegetables, tobacco and cotton.
www.migaocorp.com

Moly Mines (TSX: MOL), Market Cap: $125M
Moly Mines is an Australian resources company focused on the development of major specialty, base and precious metals projects. The company's Spinifex Ridge project, located in the Pilbara region of Western Australia, hosts a 470 million ton molybdenum and copper resource.
www.molymines.com

Neo Materials Technologies Inc (TSX: NEM), Market Cap: $451M
Neo Material Technologies Inc produces, processes and develops neo powders, rare earths and zirconium-based engineered materials and applications.
www.magnequench.com

Nuinsco Resources Ltd (TSX: NWI), Market Cap: $38M
Nuinsco Resources Ltd is a diversified mining company that has uranium, copper and gold interests in Quebec, Manitoba, Ontario, Saskatchewan and Turkey.
www.nuinsco.ca

Opel International (TSX: OPL), Market Cap: $77M
Opel International develops and markets solar panels for commercial applications and is developing a gallium arsenide microchip.
opelinc.com

Orca Exploration (TSX: ORC.B), Market Cap: $205M
Orca Exploration holds interest in a production sharing Agreement (PSA) with the Tanzania Petroleum Development

Corporation (TPDC) in Tanzania . The PSA covers production and marketing of gas from the Songo Songo gas field. The company also holds farm-in agreement for the acreage adjacent to the Songo Songo gas field.
www.orcaexploration.com

Peach Arch Entertainment (TSX: PAE), Market Cap: $40M
Peace Arch Entertainment creates, acquires and distributes feature film, television and specialty programming throughout the world, both directly and via third party licensees. Peace Arch has three operating divisions – film, television and home entertainment – with offices in Toronto, Los Angeles, New York and Vancouver.
www.peacearch.com

Points International Ltd (TSX: PTS), Market Cap: $239M
Points International Ltd is an internet software and services company that provides a portfolio of IT and management solutions to operators of consumer loyalty programs.
www.points.com

Rare Element Resources Ltd (TSX: RES), Market Cap: $19M
Rare Element Resources Ltd is a company exploring for gold and rare-earth elements (REEs). This company holds a 100% interest in the Bear Lodge property, which hosts the largest disseminated REE deposit in North America (U.S. Geological Survey Professional Paper 1049D) as well as extensive gold occurrences.

Redcorp Ventures Ltd (TSX: RDV), Market Cap: $83M
Redcorp Ventures Ltd is a mining company that holds a zinc-lead-copper property in British Columbia, a copper project in Portugal, and is producing oil and gas interests in Alberta.
www.redcorp-ventures.com

Roca Mines Inc (TSX: ROK), Market Cap: $202M
Roca Mines Inc is a mining company based in British Colombia. Roca's primary asset is the MAX Molybdenum Project.

It has been permitted and targeting for initial molybdenum concentrate production in 2007.
www.rocamines.com

Run of River Power Inc (TSX: ROR), Market Cap: $16M
Run of River Power Inc is a developer of green, environmentally friendly, renewable energy. The company operates a hydroelectric generation plant and is developing hydroelectric projects in British Columbia.
www.runofriverpower.com

Stella Jones (TSX: SJ), Market Cap: $467M
Stella Jones manufactures utility poles and railroad ties. It has grown steadily through acquisition.
www.stella-jones.com

Stratic Energy Corp (TSX: SE), Market Cap: $195M
Stratic Energy Corp is an oil and gas exploration and production company with development projects in Turkey, the U.K., Italy, Syria, Morocco, the Netherlands and Tunisia.
www.straticenergy.com

SXC Health Solutions Corp (TSX: SXC), Market Cap: $308M
SXC Health Solutions provides healthcare information technology solutions and pharmacy benefit management services to providers, payers and other participants in the pharmaceutical supply chain in the United States and Canada.
www.sxc.com

Vero Energy Inc (TSX: VRO), Market Cap: $274M
Vero Energy Inc is an oil and gas exploration and production company that explores for, develops and produces oil and gas in west-central Alberta.
www.veroenergy.ca

Victory Nickel Inc (TSX: NI), Market Cap: $86M
Victory Nickel Inc is a growth-oriented Canadian nickel company with over 660 million pounds of in-situ nickel in National In-

strument 43-101-compliant measured and indicated resources and an additional 530 million pounds of in-situ nickel in inferred resources at its Minago, Mel and Lac Rocher sulphide nickel deposits.
www.victorynickel.ca

Winstar Resource Ltd (TSX: WIX), Market Cap: $184M
Winstar Resources Ltd is an oil and gas exploration and production company that explores for, develops, and produces oil and gas in western Canada, Tunisia and Hungary.
www.winstar.ca

Zaio Corp (TSX: ZAO), Market Cap: $84M
Zaio Corp is a company developing a database of digital photographs and property values on residential properties in the United States.
www.zaio.com

* All Market Caps are as of April 2008

ACKNOWLEDGEMENTS

The writing of this book would not have been possible without the valuable help from Riel Roch-Decter, Geneviève Roch-Decter, Christine Tan and Tom Dicket. As well, the diligent support of Lien Ly, Zoe Whittall, Selena Qui, Jennie Gaffney, Vicki Tsang and Virginia Parraga in producing myriad drafts of the book, is recognized and appreciated. Thanks also to Steve Kaszas, Ron Bailey and Beryl McCallum, for their comments and helpful suggestions.

Ann Decter is a wonderful publisher at McGilligan Books. I am grateful for her assistance in bringing this book to life. Thank you also to Riel Roch-Decter for the cover. A special thank you for the diligent and meticulous editing of Lisa Foad.